Improving Work Groups:

A Practical Manual for Team Building (Revised)

Improving Work Groups:
A Practical Manual for Team Building
(Revised)

Dave Francis and Don Young

Amsterdam • Johannesburg • London
San Diego • Sydney • Toronto

Library of Congress Cataloging-in-Publication Data

Francis, Dave.
      Improving work groups: a practical manual for team building/ Dave Francis and Don Young. — Rev. ed.
      p. cm.
      Includes bibliographical references.
      ISBN 0-88390-330-X
      1. Division of labor. 2. Work groups. 3. Industrial organization.
I. Young, Don. II. Title.
HD51.F72   1992
658.4'02—dc20   92-31409
                                                   CIP

Pfeiffer & Company
8517 Production Avenue
San Diego, California 92121
(619) 578-5900
FAX (619) 578-2042

Acknowledgments

We would like to thank those who have enabled us to write this book. We have been greatly influenced by the ideas of others. The most valuable source of inspiration has been the thousands of managers who have worked with us over the past twenty years and who have shared their experiences as they grappled with the task of transforming theory into practice. A major contributor to the book was Hélène Francis, who read the manuscript and made many helpful comments. The responsibility for all errors and omissions is, of course, that of the authors.

Dave Francis
Don Young

Hove, England
July, 1992

CONTENTS

Introduction

Managers today are asking some fundamental questions about what their roles should be. No longer are military leaders the models of business-management style. Instead, management theory is being influenced by people who advocate teamwork, vision, strategic intent, trust, openness, flexibility, and participation. These concepts and values form the core of structured team building.

We think of team leadership as a distinctive management style that requires a commitment to develop the team's resources rather than a desire to control the team like a master puppeteer. Team management is neither easy nor an abdication of responsibility. It is the opposite of the political-gamester approach to management, in which the skills required are those of manipulation and control.

The effective leader builds openness, empowers others to develop their unique competencies and skills, makes the most of team members' energy, and harnesses team members' initiative. To lead a team, the leader must be able to channel individual members' energies into a collective energy.

Improving Work Groups: A Practical Manual for Team Building (revised) is a partisan book. It reflects the authors' belief that the team approach is a relevant, timely, humanistic, and effective method of getting things done. The team-management style is a positive way of managing tomorrow's organizations and of channeling the energies of those who work within them.

Leaders who use team building are guided by a clear, potent, and practical management philosophy. As a result, they develop skills that increase their subordinates' openness, commitment, and problem-solving abilities. Issues of discipline are clarified and are less likely to degenerate into "us-against-them" conflicts. As their teams' ability to self-regulate increases, team members' commitment to decisions increases. The time and effort invested in building a positive team spirit bears fruit in the form of good will.

A well-developed team, which may be the most flexible and competent tool known to organizations today, can benefit its organization with the following abilities and assets:

- ***Management of Complexity:*** The breadth of resources available within the team enables complex situations to be managed creatively.
- ***Rapid Response:*** Well-developed teams are capable of responding quickly and energetically. Team members can detect when others need help and are quick to offer support.
- ***High Motivation:*** Team membership satisfies each member's need for a feeling of personal significance, and team processes encourage activity and achievement.
- ***High-Quality Decisions:*** Mature, effective teams are capable of making better-quality decisions than all but the most brilliant individual. Different viewpoints act as checks against the biases of one person's viewpoint. Hence, the use of a team approach improves the overall quality of decision making. Perhaps more important, the level of commitment of members to team decisions is much higher.
- ***Collective Commitment:*** When team members share the processes of problem solving and decision making, they are more likely to "own" the team's plans and to do everything possible to transform plans into reality.
- ***Collective Strength:*** Individual organizational members often feel that it is difficult to influence their organizations and to make any impact outside their immediate areas. The team approach changes this; team members' perspectives and levels of influence broaden until they see that, together, they have influence and can achieve much.

The team approach is a distinctive work style whose goal is to harness team members' collective talents and energies to achieve shared objectives. Progressive, forward-thinking leaders around the world are seeking a positive management philosophy that gets results and, at the same time, respects employees' needs and capabilities. The team approach that is described in this book is designed for such progressive leaders.

Part 1:

The Team-Building Process

1

How to Use This Book

Teams and teamwork can, with proper development, be an organization's most flexible and powerful tools. *Improving Work Groups* (revised) is a practical handbook for developing the creative and productive potential of teams. As the title suggests, the book advocates a structured approach to team building and is written as a step-by-step manual.

This book is written for the person who needs practical methods for developing team effectiveness. The reader may be a facilitator, a team's leader, or a team member. Throughout this book we address our comments to "the facilitator," but leaders can (and, we believe, should) facilitate their own teams' development. The leader has a vital part to play in the development of a team approach.

In a sense, a team is a work family. A family is a human institution that shares many of the characteristics of the high-performing team.[1] Tolstoy said, "All happy families resemble one another, but each unhappy family is unhappy in its own way." This suggests that well-functioning families, like excellent companies, are good at getting the basics right.

Families connect people with the past and the future, thus providing identity and support. A good family provides love and protection. A sound family is a powerful source for its members. The best teams generate the same positive qualities that close and happy families enjoy. A healthy team, like a strong family, is a source of support and motivation—it stimulates its members to excel.

Efficient teams have six major strengths:

- Individual weaknesses are neutralized by others' strengths;
- Teamwork builds consensus and commitment to common objectives;
- Team membership is a strong motivator;

---

[1] This theme is developed further in *Unblocking Organizational Values,* by Dave Francis and Mike Woodcock, Glenview, IL: Scott, Foresman, 1990. This book is available from Pfeiffer & Company.

5

- Members can learn to work together with efficiency, effectiveness, and enjoyment;
- Teams can discipline errant members (as a result, errors and sloppy thinking are less likely to occur); and
- Teamwork skills enable people to be assimilated into new teams and to become effective quickly.

Team building is not a panacea for all organizational problems. For some self-sustaining individuals, teamwork is inappropriate. A few senior managers sound a note of caution about teamwork. For example, Peter Walters, the chairman of British Petroleum, said, "That was just one part of the personnel management claptrap which became the vogue in the 1960s. The truth was that one chap set the tone" ("Business Changes," 1983, p. 12). Even though teamwork may be desirable, it requires an open-communication style of management that not all leaders are able or willing to use.

Not all teams are effective. Several competent individuals can prove completely ineffective when they work together as a team. The team members may have different objectives, fail to share information, or lack a coordinated approach to getting things done. It is one of the great ironies of life that five people can invent a camel when trying to design a horse. Two plus two can equal negative one!

STRUCTURE OF THIS BOOK

Improving Work Groups blends diagnosis, explanation, and ideas with practical tools for building a team. The following outline clarifies the book's structure.

We begin the book by exploring team-building processes in depth with the purpose of providing a substructure of ideas for the leader. We answer four questions: What is a team? Why build teams? How should a team be built? Who builds teams? This section offers guidelines, identifies opportunities, and makes some cautionary statements.

The work-team leader is briefed on the purpose and administration of the Team-Review Survey, which is used to identify the strengths and weaknesses of a team.

The heart of the book encompasses twelve sections, one on each of the potential team blockages that are identified in the Team-Review Survey.

The activities that are included in Part Four of this book are specific suggestions to help the progress of team building. These can be thought of as tools in a tool kit. Each activity is a structured experience for the team to undertake. The activities are described in detail, with step-by-step procedures. Many can be undertaken without outside help. Through the experience gained by working through these projects, the team should gain the insight and skills needed to resolve any team blockages.

BEYOND STRUCTURE

Few teams develop to their full potential of effectiveness without nurturing and conscious development, but team building cannot be planned and predicted through a rigidly programed approach. There will be spurts of progress and apparent relapses; new insights will develop along the way; and carefully formulated programs will need to be changed. The team's experiences lead to the analysis of future needs. Competent facilitators value their feelings as much as their intellectual analyses. There is much wisdom in intuition. The team-building process is organic, evolutionary, and holistic. A special ingredient is needed that only the facilitator can add: his or her energy, insights, and skills.

Team building is a *process,* not an event. This distinction is fundamental. Team building requires a number of experiences over time. In this book we provide a framework; the facilitator oversees the implementation.

Those who facilitate team building are advised to use the frameworks and techniques on themselves before they try them on others. It is difficult to feel the power of an intervention without having been in the "hot seat" oneself. So build your own team, then go build others.

ORGANIZATIONAL BENEFITS
OF TEAM BUILDING

Organizations that succeed in the future will be those that use teamwork to be unusually innovative, creative, and bold. The challenges to today's organizations can be grouped under ten headings:

1. Challenges from increasingly strong global competitors;
2. Challenges from increasingly aggressive competition;
3. Challenges from companies that are becoming more sophisticated at market analysis and marketing;
4. Challenges from increasingly creative computer and technology systems;
5. Challenges from different values and expectations of customers and workers;
6. Challenges from the need to move away from traditional organizational structures toward new forms of corporate structures;

7. Challenges from employees' move away from lifetime employment to the perception that their careers are tapestries of different activities;
8. Challenges from the growing power of Asian and Eastern-European countries;
9. Challenges from the need to manage cultural diversity in every aspect of the organization's activities; and
10. Challenges from the need to keep organizations alive, adaptable, and flexible, but not threatening to employees.

In the future, team effectiveness will be the key to successful management. This is the era of specialists, but the more we specialize the more closely we have to work with others. Students of organizational theory emphasize that effective "linkages" between people and teams are routes to commercial success. How often have you heard the expression "the left hand doesn't know what the right hand is doing"? This is a symptom of poor teamwork.

The value of the team approach is emphasized to top managers by the U.K. Institute of Directors: "Although a private company may, in law, have one director only, it would be in general unwise to do so. The reason for this lies in the nature of the decisions directors take. Based as they are on uncertain assumptions about the future, they require the exercise of a great deal of judgment and mental weighing and testing. No more efficient method has yet been discovered for carrying out this process than discussion by a well-informed small group" *(Guidelines for Directors,* 1982).

The world will undergo major changes, many of which cannot be predicted. New competitors will emerge, predators will try to take the most attractive opportunities, and new technology will change the ways in which products and services are produced and sold. In such a challenging and volatile environment, we will find ourselves working with colleagues to find new ways of achieving world-class performance and finding the competitive edge. Teamwork is essential: it questions assumptions, generates ideas, shares problems, and coordinates effort. Only those organizations and companies that have skillful leaders who are committed to teamwork can look to the future with confidence.

REFERENCES

Business changes. (1983, December 29). *The London Daily Telegraph,* p. 12.

Guidelines for directors. (1982). London: U.K. Institute of Directors.

Team Building:
What, Why, and How

Although leaders often speak of teams and teamwork, many are vague about the precise meanings of the words. It is important to clearly understand the distinctive characteristics of a team approach.

We define a team as a high-performing task group whose members are actively interdependent and share common performance objectives. Not all groups are teams. Notice that the definition includes the expressions "high-performing," "actively interdependent," and "share common performance objectives." Although some characteristics of teamwork can be cultivated in large groups, an organization in its entirety cannot be classified as a team because its members are not actively interdependent. However, supervisors of departments—and even of whole enterprises—can adopt the team concept as their management style. After the team members and the leader have been trained and committed to the team approach, they will begin to realize that ad-hoc teams can be formed as the need arises and that the team approach can be applied outside the boundaries of their own teams.

There are times when people use their group memberships to achieve personal ends or to protect themselves. At other times, committees can stifle creativity and complicate the decision-making process. Many leaders rightly complain that meetings are a unique blend of boredom, time wasting, and muddle-headed decisions. Such ineffectual groups are not true teams. A team is more than a collection of individuals. It is, in part, an emotional entity, rooted in the feelings as well as the thoughts of its members, who actively care about their team's well-being.

According to the definition, team members are interdependent—they relate directly to one another to get things done. This suggests a practical limitation on size, because rarely in practice can more than nine people function as a single team.

It once was thought that a team was a fixed collection of people who worked together. Not so. Temporary teams often are created to solve a problem or seize an opportunity. The skills of creating and sustaining ad-hoc teams are crucial to the success of today's enterprises.

CHARACTERISTICS OF AN EFFECTIVE TEAM

While researching this book, we asked more than two thousand managers to define an effective team. We found ten characteristics that were almost universally named. We will explore the main conclusions from our survey in the following pages.

Many of the managers recognized that effective teams skillfully combine appropriate individual talents with a positive team spirit to achieve results. Some of the characteristics named are paradoxical and seem to contradict one another. This is, in fact, true: effective teamwork is the synthesis of apparently contrary forces.

Characteristic 1: Conflict

It is widely thought that effective teams are harmonious and unified. Not so. Excessive harmony can encourage intellectual dishonesty. Challenge, openness, and veracity among team members is an essential characteristic of team effectiveness.

Characteristic 2: Discipline

There comes a time when teams need to do what they are told. This is true even at the most senior levels of government. After a policy has been agreed on by a senior group, implementation is mandatory; the team has to play its allotted part. Imagine what would happen if the brass section in a symphony orchestra decided to play "When the Saints Come Marching In" during Beethoven's Fifth Symphony.

Characteristic 3: Energy

In an effective team, members gain strength from one another. Collectively, they feel more potent and find that team activities renew their vitality and enjoyment. The word "synergy" was coined to describe this special group energy. Synergy has been explained with this mathematically improbable, but psychologically accurate, equation: $2 + 2 = 5$. A team's power goes beyond the sum of its individual members. A team has the capacity for synergy—a group energy that can deliberately be developed and utilized.

Characteristic 4: Learning

Effective team members continually learn better ways of working together. They review their experiences in order to critique both individual and team performance. Interestingly, teams operate like organisms; in a way, they learn regardless of who the members are.

Characteristic 5: Methodology

Teams often are required to solve problems and make decisions. A shared methodology of problem solving is an essential discipline. Often, innovative solutions are needed, so teams need to be genuinely creative.

Characteristic 6: Objectives

Every team needs a purpose that is understood, shared, and considered worthwhile by its members. This purpose can be described as the team's *mission*. Teams derive their objectives from their missions. Objectives take the form both of broad team objectives and of specific objectives for each member. Teams draw strength and direction from a deep, shared understanding of common purpose and from an understanding of how each member's objectives contribute to the achievement of the team's broader purpose.

Characteristic 7: Output

The "acid test" of a team is its capacity to deliver the goods. High standards are essential. A team is capable of achieving results (both in quality and quantity) that its members cannot achieve in isolation. Team members' diverse talents combine to create end products that are beyond individual members' capabilities.

Characteristic 8: Structure

A mature team has dealt with thorny questions about control, leadership, procedures, organization, and roles. The team's structure is finely attuned to the tasks that are undertaken. Individual talents and contributions are utilized without confusion. Team members with a drive for leadership have learned to understand one another and to cope with any feelings of hostility, competitiveness, or aggression. Mature teams are flexible, responsive, orderly, and directed.

Characteristic 9: Mutual Support

Members of an effective team develop a distinctive team spirit that encourages mutual respect, support, and simple enjoyment of one another. Team members identify themselves with their team. Team success or failure affects each member, and the members will extend themselves to serve the interests of the team. Effective teams have an atmosphere that supports confidence sharing, effective listening, problem solving, and risk taking.

Characteristic 10: Team-Member Fulfillment

High-performing teams look after their members in more ways than through providing a menu of psychological rewards. Team members actually grow in stature through their membership. Their potential is recognized and developed.

WHAT IS TEAM BUILDING?

Learning is generally thought of as an individual pursuit, but this is only partially true. Teams also learn, and their collective skills belong to the group as a whole. Watch a professional football game or an astronaut crew and you will see highly advanced team ability.

The process of deliberately creating an effective team is called team building. The expression is useful because it suggests that something substantial has to be constructed and that the process will go through several stages and take time to complete. This elusive but crucial level of collective learning is the core of team building.

Team building involves the deliberate working through of all blockages to progress until a work group becomes an effective team. The idea of clearing blockages (which is more extensively developed in later chapters) is the most important tool in our approach to team building. If a blockage is worked through successfully, the team becomes stronger. If the blockage is not cleared, the team regresses. Another important idea is expressed by the term "working through," because time and focused effort are required to resolve blockages.

STAGES OF TEAM DEVELOPMENT

Teams have a process of growth that can be understood and described, although the stages of team development do not follow a predictable, step-by-step evolutionary sequence. Nonetheless, a clear pattern can be detected as a loose assembly of people goes through the developmental obstacle course and emerges as a team.

Teams need care at every phase of their evolution. New teams have much to learn; they must clarify roles, build relationships, and develop effective processes. Each change of role prompts a need to review the team.

Even well-established teams cannot rest on their laurels; they need to address the risks of excessive arrogance, self-satisfaction, and the poor decision making that can result.

We have identified four distinct stages of team development. These are:

Stage 1: Testing

People react very differently to the prospect of meeting new colleagues. Some are fearful and have sweaty palms and dry lips. Others are eager, looking forward to opportunities for excitement, achievement, and challenge. Some may be evasive, disgruntled, attention seeking, or morose. The possibilities are endless.

It is with this foundation that the team begins to form. New members initially try to find their places in the group. Their psychological antennae are fully attuned to subtle, nonverbal messages. Each new member tries, in his or her own way, to answer the question, "How (or where) do I belong to this group?," and interacts with the other members in the way in which he or she feels most comfortable. For example, some people hang back and observe until they feel comfortable, while others jump right in with a sense of humor and amiable conversation.

As the team begins to coalesce, there is a gradual growth of exchange and contact. People begin to find out about one another's attitudes, values, styles, and readiness to be contacted. This testing process continues until each person makes a decision concerning the nature of his or her involvement.

At this stage, the team may appear to be acting effectively, progressing with its tasks, and forming what seems to be a friendly comradeship among members. However, this condition often is only skin deep, because the team's initial effectiveness stems from attitudes and training that were in place prior to the team's being formed. For a team to mature, its members must get to know one another in a less superficial way. As a result, the members' initial feelings of comfort may dissipate as deeper issues rise to the surface.

Stage 2: Infighting

As the team develops, its members deal with the issues of power and influence. Alliances are formed and certain people emerge as particularly significant. The leader has particular authority because the organization has recognized his or her significant contribution. Still, this position must be earned in the eyes of the team members, who watch and evaluate the leader's behavior. They may accept their leader's leadership or they may find cunning ways to evade it.

At this stage, the team has to decide how it is going to operate. All too often, this is done by subterranean evolution but with little explicit planning. In essence, all of the issues are concerned with control. Three questions are dominant:

1. Who controls the team?
2. How is control exercised?
3. What happens to "delinquents"?

The team has to find an answer to each of these questions if it is to develop. There are no easy answers or "quick fixes." Difficulties that face the team will be either confronted or evaded. Some teams fail to work through their control issues; this permanently blocks them and, although they may appear to make progress, underneath there is a fundamental weakness.

Stage 3: Getting Organized

Following the successful resolution (for the time being, at least) of its control issues, the team begins to tackle its work with a new energy. At this stage, the team members want to work together and have committed themselves to making the team an effective one. The team needs the support and interest of all of its members. Without them, individual preoccupations dominate, and the team will be unable to grow stronger.

The work of the team needs to be identified exactly as each member's contribution is discussed and measured. Typically, the quality of listening improves, and people begin to respect one another. Team members become concerned with economy of effort and task effectiveness and they become effective at solving problems and making decisions. A shared methodology of problem solving is developed. The team members learn to:

- Tune in to problems and assess the challenges posed;
- Explore, clarify, and set objectives;
- Clarify criteria for achieving success and techniques for measuring success;
- Collect and structure information and devise options for action;
- Evaluate options for action;
- Develop effective plans and a strategy for carrying them out;
- Take intelligent and effective action; and
- Review to learn and improve their performance.

At this stage the team has to grow in its capacity to handle problems creatively, flexibly, and effectively. Without this evolution of working methods, the team will continue to use barely effective modes of operating, satisfying itself with adequate effectiveness rather than striving for excellence.

Getting organized takes time. A depth of understanding among team members needs to be developed, and approaches to problem solving need to be shared, so that structured methods of operating are established and objectives are rigorously clarified.

Stage 4: Mature Closeness

The members of a fully established team develop rapport and closeness. Sometimes these feelings are so strong that strong bonds of comradeship are forged. Team members are willing to extend themselves for their colleagues, and a genuine enjoyment of one another is typical.

Disciplined informality, which is based on mutual respect, often is the *modus operandi* of a team at this stage. There is a strong feeling that others are willing to help if needed. Team members' roles have been identified, and each person's contribution is distinctive and valued.

Although the team members' close bonds may be evident to outsiders, the team members also build relationships with those outside the team. Aware that it is difficult to prevent the development of rumors and negative images, team members take steps to reduce the risk that their closeness will lead to arrogance and insular attitudes.

A mature team takes steps to clarify its role in the organization. It does not allow its function to become redundant or obscure; it will influence others to provide the necessary recognition and support.

A team at this advanced stage of development shows the following:

- *High energy* (members feel positive and motivated);
- *Attention to tasks* (care, objectivity and hard work);
- *Shared values* (common basic beliefs in what is important);
- *Openness* (willingness to consider new information and different viewpoints);
- *Confrontation* (constructive use of conflict);
- *Trust* (belief that its members take one another's interests seriously and that people will fulfill their promises); and
- *Enjoyment* (taking pleasure in being part of the team).

MOTIVES FOR TEAM BUILDING

It is important to understand the motives that leaders of teams have for initiating team-building ventures. The following are some examples of motives for which team building is appropriate:

- A newly appointed leader wants to achieve rapid progress.
- A pragmatic leader wants to use team building to further an open, problem-solving approach to management.
- A leader who faces new challenges needs the creativity and commitment of all those involved to handle the task.
- A leader who faces problems related to relationships, commitment, or lack of clarity needs to break out of the doldrums.

Team building sometimes is undertaken for more negative reasons, and the results frequently are disappointing. For example:

- Team building may be initiated by an edict from the corporate headquarters and may not have the support of those who are directly involved.
- A leader may undertake team building with the intention of increasing his or her capacity to manipulate and control. This is contrary to the values that are the foundation of the team-building approach.

The process of teaming people to achieve a goal that matters to them is central to the team approach. Whenever possible, a team-building program should be implemented only after all members of the team have agreed to undertake the required developmental steps. If this is not the case, the team-building efforts can do more harm than good. Team-building techniques are powerful and can be abused. The decision should be made without pressure but with sufficient information. In practice, we have seen no ill effects when groups have applied our techniques on the basis of voluntary participation.

WHO CAN BENEFIT FROM TEAM BUILDING?

Team building is time consuming and can be expensive. It is important to identify the benefits of the team-building approach. We will review the benefits of team building to strategic teams, management teams, management-development specialists, project teams, individuals, work groups, and ad-hoc task groups.

Strategic Teams

Teams that are supervised by top managers often are the major links between an organization and its external environment. These teams must assess the environment, predict the effects of new forces on the organization, and make tough decisions about the organization's strategy. These tasks require far-sighted and imaginative appraisals of complex issues that are beyond the scope of one person working alone.

A for-profit organization faces special challenges. It must determine a winning competitive strategy that provides focus to the business and superior value to the customer. This strategy must be built deep into the fabric of the organization so that it is difficult for competitors to replicate. Top managers must ensure that broad goals are translated into energetic and focused activity. Unless they are handled well, the political issues of top-management groups can be extremely destructive to the well-being of the organization.

Management Teams

Management teams—usually individual managers and their subordinates—are the most common foci of team-building initiatives. Such teams are relatively stable and handle a wide variety of assignments (e.g., running a factory, department, or service facility). The quality of relationships among team members can affect large numbers of people who look to the team for clear and energetic direction.

The essential quality of a management team is that there is a high degree of interdependence. The team often will comprise various functional specialists, each of whom contributes a distinctive type of expertise. The leader builds the specialists into a mature and competent team, sets the overall team agenda, and manages the team's process (how it operates).

Management-Development Specialists

Those who are responsible for developing an organization's managerial resources continually seek ways to broaden ideas, develop useful skills, and encourage an assertive, strategically focused, positive approach to management. Management-development specialists can find many useful ideas and techniques in team-building technology. By acquiring a team perspective, the management developer is intervening at two levels: the sociological (team) level and the psychological (individual) level. The team-building approach usually receives little resistance from managers because they recognize that it has the potential to benefit them directly in their jobs.

Management-development specialists can develop themselves as trainers in team-building methods and as facilitators to managers who are using team-building techniques with their own teams. This strengthens the specialist's role, gives practical relevance to his or her work, and provides a defined yet flexible framework to guide the management-development process.

We have seen team building "take off" in many large organizations, focusing the development of management skills and giving new vitality to personnel and management-development advisors. Unlike more individualistic or mechanistic approaches to development, the team-building approach is readily accepted and "owned" by managers who achieve further development as a result of their own energy and initiative.

Project Teams

Many organizations are using project or ad-hoc teams to solve problems quickly and to develop new processes or products. Such teams may exist for a few weeks or for years at a time. Project teams can be developed into a distinct organizational form (the "adhocracy"). Project teams are frequently responsible for achieving specific objectives, and the team-building approach offers major benefits.

It is necessary for project managers to assemble teams whose members possess both the mix of skills that technically can handle the project and a variety of personality types. Project managers must create enough drive and enthusiasm to see the project through. Difficult decisions often have to be made on uncertain data, and a well-developed team can use the diverse talents of team members in making effective decisions. This form of decision making, so well displayed by early members of the Apollo space program, has significant advantages. Team-building techniques are relevant—probably essential—in enabling project teams to work effectively.

For example, an electronics organization obtained an order for a $50 million radar installation that had to be completed within a tight two-year time frame. All of the senior project managers met off site for a one-week team-building session, during which they identified more than one hundred problems and planned appropriate corrective measures. Such organizational issues could not have emerged while the technical problems of day-to-day operations predominated. After the session, the managers agreed that "the team-building workshop doesn't make the job easy, but it does make it possible."

Individual Team Members

Individual team members develop their personal skills through team-building experiences. They become more competent in working with others to solve problems effectively. Team building broadens the concept of leadership and gives team members the opportunity to practice developing a supportive, open climate.

We know of one competent technical manager who was assigned to head a major subsidiary a few weeks after he went through a team-building session. After six months he said, "If I had not experienced the team-building session, I would have handled the assignment entirely differently. I set up project and review teams all over the place, whereas previously I would have dealt with individuals separately. Now I have their commitment."

Representative Teams and Committees

Committee members represent interest groups or are appointed to contribute particular skills or viewpoints. In part, their function is defensive: to see that their home groups are not damaged and, preferably, are enhanced. Additionally, members are expected to contribute to the committee's task, which may be complex or difficult.

Commitment from members may be difficult to obtain because committees often are temporary. It is not an accident that the word "committee" so frequently produces a negative emotional reaction. Committees can be ponderous, ineffective, and maddening; yet effective representative groups are necessary to coordinate areas of common interest.

Committees need to be developed as teams in order to overcome the partisan interests of their members. Team-building techniques are especially valuable when used with committees and temporary teams, as they bring latent issues to the surface and clear them before they become blockages.

Work Groups

Since the recognition of the importance of a team approach in the workplace (e.g., by the quality-circles movement), theories of motivation have been developed to try to counter the indifference and lack of care that affects many production and service units. One solution is to use a team concept at the "shop-floor" level. This emphasizes participation and more workplace democracy, with the overall aim of channeling people's creative energy toward benefiting the organization rather than toward blocking its progress. The leader's role evolves from *directing* the team's work to *facilitating* it.

Beginning the
Team-Building Process

In general, change occurs because someone makes a positive intervention. In team building, a "midwife" is needed to facilitate the process with energy and insight. This person may be the team's leader, a team member, or an internal or external facilitator. (A discussion of whether to select a professional facilitator is presented in the next chapter.)

Team building is a process of development and change. Those involved need to have a personal theory of how to accomplish change effectively. This is especially relevant for the person who is serving as the facilitator. The term "a theory of change" may create unwarranted tension in people who fear that they will have to absorb the contents of bulky tomes with titles such as *A Technical Psychopathology of Organizational Dynamics*. Not true. The most valuable data comes from personal experience—information that has been learned in one's own environment. A personal theory of change needs to be expressed in terms that people can understand. As you read the next few pages, think through your own approach, clarify the elements of that approach, and begin to build your personal theory.

Leader Development: Robin

At only thirty years of age, Robin had moved up the corporate ladder rapidly. He was selected to direct a small team in developing a promising new market. But after a few months, his immediate staff members were vehement in their criticism of his performance. They claimed that, protected by a well-groomed secretary, he brooded in his satinwood office, dictated notes to his staff, and asked for endless jobs to be accomplished at once.

Soon after receiving one of Robin's impeccably typed and grammatically perfect notes, a subordinate would be subject to pointed inquiries as to why the myriad of assigned tasks had not been accomplished. His staff said that Robin's clipped, precise manner defined the world in terms that he could understand but that excluded the viewpoints of everyone else. Robin was aware of his difficulties, but he reacted by becoming more involved in detail and by trying to intensify his image as a dynamic, cavalier young leader.

After a colleague suggested that Robin have an open discussion with his team, a team-building session was planned. Robin and his group discussed the issues very openly. When his subordinates expressed their honest opinions, Robin was shocked. Seeking an explanation, Robin talked about his background. He was a scientist who had spent his youth learning obscure facts about protons and antimatter particles. The scientific method had been his discipline, and lonely study had been his means of accomplishment. This method of work became habitual; it led to a good academic degree and, with slight adjustments, produced many achievements in market research.

In the team-building session, Robin realized that he was using acquired attitudes that were appropriate in a science laboratory but were infuriating and ineffective in a corporate environment. For Robin, professional development meant learning to share doubts, possibilities, and decisions with others and to deal with the emotional as well as the intellectual issues in his group.

Leader Development: May

May was the leader of a group of construction planners. She was amiable, considerate, diligent, and concerned about her team's problems. However, her team members were not happy. They were ineffective, and their inability to work together was a standing joke. Projects had slow and painful births and wallowed through the successive stages of development. Somehow the team always managed to avoid humiliation with a frenzied burst of "emergency repair" at the eleventh hour.

At first, this process of indulgence followed by frantic, last-minute activity was fun, but it eventually became so disturbing that the group members became frustrated. All expressions of discontent were openly expressed and, apparently, were seriously considered. Yet nothing was done because the group had poor decision-making skills. May had read so many books on participative management that she felt uncomfortable about assuming the decision-making role. Her desire to encourage ideas and maintain close group relationships was realized at the expense of clear planning and effective utilization of resources.

The team-building experience provided May with information about structured group problem-solving methodologies. With the help of the team, May studied her own work methods and learned to recognize when her team was getting stuck. The team members learned that they were *collectively* responsible for effective teamwork and began to set aside time to review their performance. This practice became a tradition and probably accounted for the major part of the qualitative improvement that was noticed within May's group in succeeding months.

The Process of Team Change

Robin and May began to manage their teams differently after they began to understand themselves and their roles as leaders more clearly. Each of them went through the following process of change:

- They were open to behave in different ways;
- Feedback from their groups enabled them to perceive their behavior more objectively, and needs for change were identified;
- New insights, experiences, and behaviors were examined, tried, and reviewed; and
- New ways of functioning as leaders were implemented and practiced.

It is often said that practice makes perfect. It is more accurate to say that although practice does not necessarily make perfect, it certainly makes permanent. Behaviors prompt reactions that justify attitudes that, in turn, stimulate repeat behavior. This cycle is repeated frequently and will be changed only by a definite, permanent change in the initial behavior.

STEPS IN MANAGING CHANGE

A step-by-step approach can help a team to work methodically, thereby preventing the omission of important stages in the change-management process. Our observations have led us to identify five steps that are important in managing change:

1. A desire to improve;
2. Identification of the problem and the needs for improvement;
3. Specification of the preferred situation (a vision of a better future);
4. Planned strategies and tactics for improvement; and
5. Periodic reviews of progress.

Each of these five steps is discussed in more detail below.

Step 1: A desire to improve. Change does not stem from complacency and comfort. Instead, effective change begins with the realization that all is not well (perhaps that hazards lurk ahead) or that opportunities exist that could be exploited to one's advantage. At this initial stage, feelings play an important part because the need for change must be recognized and understood by those whose opinions carry weight in the organization.

Step 2: Identification of the problem and the needs for improvement. Some team blockages can be difficult to identify. A leader who is trying to diagnose such problems can be likened to a television technician who is attempting to repair a set with an intermittent problem. The source of the problem cannot be traced until the set actually goes "bad." Usually, it would appear that Murphy's Law is in effect, because the television works perfectly while the technician is watching. Because the technician is unable to observe the symptoms, he or she often will make a superficial assessment that fails to identify the true cause of the problem. A technical analysis of the problem needs to be supplemented by the recognition of its importance. Likewise, with work teams, it sometimes is helpful for an external consultant to assist in the recognition of team blockages.

Step 3: Specification of the preferred situation. Managing organizational and team change is much like undertaking a journey: it is important to clarify where you wish to go before setting out. If you can visualize the changes you wish to see and the hazards that may stand in your way, you stand a better chance of persevering and achieving. One way of doing this is to project your imagination forward and ask yourself the question, "What precisely do I want to see happening with this team in one year?"

Most people respond to this question by censoring their visions by worrying about practical difficulties. However, at this stage it helps to ignore the practical limitations; they often exist only in one's mind rather than in the reality of the situation.

Concentrating on what you wish to have happen will help you to create a vision of the future. Others in your team also should clarify their images; then you can explore the visions and hopes that you hold in common.

Step 4: Planned strategies and tactics for improvement. After the team's vision of the future has been clarified, it should be honed until it can be expressed in terms of objectives. This is important because visions can be slippery and insubstantial. The products of imagination need to be captured and solidified or, like hobgoblins and ghosts, they will vanish with the dawn.

After objectives have been stated, strategies and tactics for their achievement can be explored. There are many treatments for team and organizational ailments, and not all can be administered at once. An appropriate treatment is one that is affordable and that is most likely to be effective.

Step 5: Periodic reviews of progress. Habits and traditions become ingrained in organizational culture. Because it is so easy to slip back and lose impetus or direction, change efforts need to be monitored. Progress can be reviewed by using mechanisms such as regular meetings, clearly defined and stated responsibilities, open discussion, and outside people (consultants) who act as mirrors to reflect the group's behavior. These monitoring devices are not restricted to team-building interventions alone. Team building can gain much from the same disciplines that leaders use in other areas, as similar standards of professionalism are required.

MANAGING THE TEAM-BUILDING PROCESS

Openness

All team members should be aware that the team-building process demands openness and that, consequently, critical comments or negative feelings may come to the surface. One leader describes the process as "lifting the stones and letting the nasties crawl out." Team building does not create "nasties," but it does give them a voice with which to express themselves. On such occasions, each team member is vulnerable, but the most vulnerable person is the leader, who usually has to cope with more criticism than anyone else. Therefore, the leader is also the person who needs to be most conscious of the process to be used and the probable outcomes of that process. It is important that he or she has a clear understanding of the values that underlie team building and the techniques and requirements of the team-building process.

The leaders who seem to respond best to team building are those who already practice openness in their relationships with others and who want to get things done *with* the team (not *to* the team). Such leaders are looking for a vehicle to manage team change more effectively and are keen to use team building for this purpose.

AVOIDING BLOWUPS

It is vital that team issues be explored constructively and creatively. Occasionally team-building sessions become tedious and dull while the team works through complicated issues. In some cases, however, team-building events can "blow up" with uncomfortable or damaging incidents. Fortunately, such cases are rare.

If group difficulties and blowups are handled with care, they can lead to significant progress. Sometimes the seeds of a breakthrough grow out of a particularly difficult group struggle. If things go wrong, it is best to deal with the incident in an open and straightforward manner and to help the team to work through the situation thoroughly. The leader's attention to the following guidelines will help to maximize the constructive value of the team-building approach.

1. Make involvement voluntary. Ensure that each team member not only understands in theory what is to happen but also has freely agreed to be involved in the session. The team-building process should be discussed before it is set in motion. It is essential to develop clear and honorable "contracts" among the facilitator and the team members.

2. Allow adequate discussion time. When a team-building effort is undertaken, allow sufficient time for all members to express themselves and to consider one another's reactions. Avoid leaving issues that have not been discussed fully.

3. Sequence events appropriately. Begin team building with more impersonal assignments, approaching more personal or controversial issues in manageable steps.

4. Use care in preparation. Care should be taken to ensure that the team-building site is comfortable and private and that the required materials are provided. Effective preparation is more likely if one person is designated the organizer/administrator.

5. Make the team's choices relevant. Each team has its own history and style. As some team-building processes work superbly for some teams but fail for others, the choice of approach is crucial. The team itself is its best arbiter, and it needs to spend time designing its program of change.

6. Avoid threatening activities. Any activity that is perceived as threatening can be hurtful or provoke aggression. Therefore, possibly threatening team-building processes are acceptable only if they are undertaken by a skilled facilitator with constructive intentions. Of course, only the team itself can decide whether an activity poses a threat to any of its members. Before a team undertakes a team-building activity that could bring out hidden information, it is essential that all members understand the likely course of events.

7. Work through conflicts and difficulties. Because difficult situations require thorough resolution, every effort should be made to avoid leaving a program unfinished. It is better to get perspectives and guidance from outside resources than it is to flounder. If you are at all uncertain about your ability to conduct a team-building program, find an experienced facilitator and enlist his or her aid. A trained team-building facilitator can greatly aid a team throughout the entire team-building process.

8. Remember that team building must be work oriented. Sometimes facilitators become interested in group dynamics or psychotherapy and seek to apply those concepts in team-building sessions. This is, in our view, unethical. There is a clear distinction between team building (which is a management technique used to promote group effectiveness) and group therapy (which is an emotional learning experience for group members).

RESOURCES

Team building involves more than a commitment of intent. Resources—primarily time and money—will be required. The chief resource needed for team building is time—time for experiencing, for giving and receiving feedback, for learning, for skill development, and for thinking through all the factors that influence the team. Some of this time should be taken from the normal working day because it is important that new practices are absorbed into the team's way of life. It is also likely that the team members will need to take time away from the working environment and to spend several days working together on their issues. Some teams find that a weekend offers the only opportunity for their members to work together uninterrupted. An offsite team-building session can have unplanned advantages as well, as demonstrated by the members of a group who met at a hotel. After working through a full day's agenda, the members adjourned to the bar. They talked about boats, children, and cars until two in the morning. Then one team member suggested that they continue the team-building session with each person's objective evaluations of the other members. There followed one of the frankest interchanges imaginable, which the group later said had been the most valuable part of the experience. Such an in-depth and productive exchange would have been difficult to engineer during normal working hours. Because of the speed at which the mix of informality and concentrated working sessions can move a team forward, the investment in an off-site location and in the extra free time often is well worth it.

The other required resource for team building is money. Team building can be undertaken cheaply if those concerned are prepared to put in extra work. Organizations can adapt imaginative team-building techniques so that little direct expenditure is required. (For example, many of the team-building activities described in this book can be undertaken without the assistance of a professional facilitator.) However, it often speeds the process if the money is spent on getting the team-building activities moving. The principal expenses are for off-site meetings (especially if the participants will be staying overnight) and for the services of a facilitator.

Team-building facilitators usually are trained in the behavioral sciences, and their job is to help the group to diagnose its ills and to resolve its blockages. Their skills and experience give confidence and pace to the process, but facilitators can only help the team-building process along. The actual work should be done by the team members themselves. The notion that every leader should have the capacity to develop effective teams (without the need for an external facilitator) has much to commend it.

SELECTING THE PARTICIPANTS

Before beginning the team-building process, it is necessary to decide who should participate and who should not. Sometimes this selection process is straightforward. For example, a team might be defined as all managers at the Newark factory or all of the technicians who are responsible for module B of the Lion project.

On the other hand, defining the membership of the team can become a fuzzy and blurred issue. Teams form and reform into different groupings as tasks change and personal relationships develop. As a new member's contribution becomes significant and previously important people draw back, boundaries become fluid. Deciding the membership of the group also may be a sensitive political issue. As status may well be affected by membership, people's personal pride is at stake. There is no simple formula for establishing boundary lines in every case. However, it can be helpful for those who control team members' participation to consider the following three levels of membership:

1. Core team members. Their contribution is necessary over an extended period, and significant reorganization would be necessary should one of them withdraw.

2. Supportive team members. Their contribution aids the team in doing its work effectively. These people are not essential for performing core tasks or for sparking creative effort. Rather, their contribution is to "pave the way"; to support others; and to provide assistance, raw materials, or information.

3. Temporary team members. Their contribution is specific and time-bound. It may be that a particular assignment requires skills that the regular team members do not possess. An outsider then may be made a temporary team member while his or her special contribution is required. The temporary team member withdraws and ceases to be a team member when his or her assignment is completed.

Using these three levels of team membership as guidelines, it becomes possible to consider each contributor to the team effort in relation to his or her function in the team and to clarify his or her position. In cases in which a team contributor should not or cannot attend a team-building session, it is helpful to discuss the issue with the person concerned and with the members of the core team.

If team building is being undertaken as part of a program of change that stretches across an entire organization, the structured methodology described in this book can be used as a "plank" of such a program. Our method does not require a mechanical sequence of development, which so many leaders find artificial and awkward. Rather, we provide tools and depend on the team to use its creativity in finding the tools that suit its needs.

TEAM-BUILDING PROCESSES

Team building can be a rather obscure and confusing technique to many leaders. It helps to have a written statement of preliminary objectives, which are checked at an early point with the team as a whole. One objective for many teams is the development of a common vision or strategy that determines where the team is going. It often is helpful for teams to develop a "charter"—a mission statement for the team. Although the task may seem contrived, it focuses the collective mind of the team on the ideal. This mission statement should include an assessment of the kinds of forces that are impacting on the group and the ideal shape of things to come.

Here is an example of an actual team's charter; the team members oversee the operation of an Ontario, Canada factory that manufactures light fixtures.

We will:

- Develop systematic and comprehensive information-gathering processes;
- Spend quality time brainstorming ideas;
- Develop a formal control mechanism (a team coordinator to structure team work and ensure that conflict is dealt with constructively;
- Circulate an agenda prior to all team meetings;
- Ensure that we get to know one another as people;
- Ask a third party to monitor our work from time to time to ensure that we are working effectively;
- Ensure that strict time-management procedures are adopted;
- Ensure that each meeting ends with a critical review for improvement;
- Give everyone "air time"; and
- Take meeting notes and distibute them to all team members within three days.

It sometimes happens that issues raised in team-building sessions are too deep for immediate assessment or require further information. One of the important outcomes of a team-building session is the identification of the mechanisms with which the group will continue to work on unresolved issues. These should be worked on, clarified, and solved as part of the normal working process of the team. Some objectives will deal with tasks, some with team organization, and some with team processes.

ORGANIZATION-WIDE DEVELOPMENT

It is true that organization-wide problems require organization-wide solutions. However, massive organizational-change programs often resemble military campaigns in hostile terrain, requiring extensive reserves of trained troops. Unfortunately, such grand projects frequently fail and become sour recollections of lost opportunities.

Although it is almost impossible for any outsider to energize a large organization and keep it moving, it is possible for a consultant to provide the spark that activates the organization's latent energy and to channel its expression. If organization-wide development is being considered, it is important to seek professional advice before making a major commitment. (Information on choosing a professional consultant is provided in the next chapter.)

THE EFFECTS OF CHANGE ON TEAMS

To a point, a team is capable of remaining effective despite changes in its membership. Effective teams have methods of introducing new people and giving them the repertoire of skills, knowledge, and attitudes that are required for them to play effective roles. To some extent, a team is capable of sustaining its learning and development despite changes in its membership. However, rapid changes of membership put a special stress on the capacity of the team. In particular, it is well known that a change of leader has profound effects on the team.

A word of caution is an appropriate way to conclude this chapter. Team building can unbalance an organization. To illustrate, the senior members of a group in a large food factory prided themselves on being ahead of the pack. They used the most advanced techniques available for production control, manufacturing, and personnel development. They then decided to self-administer team-building techniques. After a number of sessions were held, the members became closer and more competent. They went out of their way to keep one another informed and, almost to the point of compulsion, planned joint projects with their own blend of creativity, order, and energy. The site manager was delighted, saying that "this team building has affected us more fundamentally than anything else we've tried." Several months later, the situation in the factory had changed. According to the site manager, "The team building worked, but it worked too well. We put a lot of extra effort into our senior group, and this left the next level down feeling more isolated and out of things. Our effectiveness has really deteriorated."

Components of a system are interdependent. When one is changed, others are affected. If one team is built at the expense of another, a string of negative reactions may ensue. It is impossible to forecast all the effects of change; thus, requiring absolute certainty of outcome before undertaking a new project is a recipe for failure. However, it is necessary and wise to look ahead and to try to spot the potential dangers.

Facilitating the
Team-Building Process

Improving Work Groups is a "do-it-yourself" book. We have designed the book so that most leaders of teams will be able to use it without the assistance of an outside facilitator. However, there are some circumstances in which teams will benefit from external help.

This chapter provides practical guidelines for choosing and working with a facilitator. The following issues will be addressed:

- When to use a facilitator;
- What external and internal facilitators can contribute to the team-building process;
- The qualities and characteristics of an effective team-building facilitator;
- Where to find a good facilitator;
- How to choose a suitable facilitator; and
- The stages of working with a facilitator.

WHEN TO USE A FACILITATOR

A facilitator can be of great benefit to an inexperi-enced team that is beginning a process of team building. Initially, there is the natural apprehension of the team's leaders and members in setting out on an uncharted course. Leaders may feel particularly exposed, especially if they suspect that "nasties" may lurk beneath the surface. Some team members may feel apprehensive about revealing their true feelings during a new and unfamiliar process. For the inexperienced team, the facilitator acts as a coach, guide, and mentor.

As their skills develop, teams usually become adept at recognizing their own team-process problems. But at first, team members may be unable to stand back and see what is really going on; so the perspective of an external facilitator provides the necessary objectivity. While a team is developing, problems and issues may arise that are particularly difficult or sensitive; these call for the skills of a facilitator.

As a team matures, it develops the ability to handle its own problems. However, there is always the danger of complacency. Mature and effective teams may want to spend time with a trusted facilitator once or twice a year just to get another perspective on how things are going.

The following questions are helpful in deciding whether to use a facilitator:

- Are you about to start a team-building process with an inexperienced team?
- Does the leader have the skills to manage the team-building process?
- Are there are difficult or sensitive issues to be worked through?
- Do team members feel that they are too involved in the issues to be able to stand back and see what is going on?
- Would it be helpful to receive impartial feedback on team performance and blockages?
- Are the team members so close that they may have lost their objectivity toward one another?
- Are there intergroup problems that are difficult for the team to handle alone?

If you answered "yes" to any of these questions, an external facilitator is likely to be helpful.

EXTERNAL AND INTERNAL FACILITATORS

Some facilitators work within the organization ("internals"), while others act as consultants ("externals"). Both types of facilitators bring advantages and disadvantages to the organizations that they serve.

Internal facilitators are likely to be very knowledgeable about the organization, committed to long-term interventions, and personally trusted. However, internal facilitators may be perceived as cautious (their "heads are on the block"), lacking in skills, or low in status.

External facilitators are less likely to be knowledgeable about the organization, to be committed to long-term interventions, and to be trusted personally. However, external facilitators may be perceived as highly skilled, impartial, and high in status.

THE FACILITATOR'S ROLE

Neither an external nor an internal facilitator can make a team effective; teams must do that for themselves. There is no instance in which a facilitator should do the work of the team. However, a facilitator can assist a team in many different ways. A facilitator helps the team to accomplish ten objectives:

1. Establish a positive climate for team building;
2. Structure the process of team building;
3. Collect (and make sense of) valid data on how the team is functioning;
4. Set team-building objectives;
5. Establish criteria so that team building can be monitored;
6. Identify blockages to effective work processes;
7. Diagnose what is going on in the team and why the blockages exist;
8. Recognize, confront, and work through team blockages;
9. Develop a shared vision of the future that will guide further team-building efforts; and
10. Establish concrete action plans for continued progress.

By openly and constructively aiding the team in achieving these ten objectives, the facilitator serves as a role model. The facilitator should take every opportunity to demonstrate constructive ways to assist the team in identifying its strengths, aid the team in identifying and confronting blockages to effectiveness, guide the team in clarifying the roles it should play, and help the team plan to improve.

A team-building facilitator should *not:*

- Usurp leadership. Rather, he or she should support the leader and each team member.
- Tell the team what is wrong with it. Instead, the facilitator should help the team to recognize its problems.
- Make decisions for the team. The facilitator's role is to help the team to make its own decisions.
- Become involved in the content of the team's work. Facilitators should focus on the *process* of the team's *modus operandi.*
- Make the team dependent on his or her continued presence. Instead, he or she should work to make the team independent of external help.
- Use the team as a therapy group. Team-building facilitators should concentrate on task effectiveness.

Effective facilitators are skilled in working with groups of people in a sensitive, supportive way and in dealing with work teams' problems. These are the skills and experience for which the team is paying.

CHARACTERISTICS OF AN EFFECTIVE TEAM-BUILDING FACILITATOR

We know of a brilliant facilitator who failed high school, worked as a carpenter for fifteen years, and then by accident became involved in team-building work. Another successful facilitator started work as an engineer and, through his church membership, became involved in social work and then team building. Another colleague has a degree in psychology and a Ph.D. from a dissertation on psychotherapeutic research. One of the worst failures we have encountered in the consulting business has a degree in sociology and long experience in social work, clinical psychology, and research. Clearly, no single avenue of training or background is best for someone who plans to become a facilitator.

Because of the diversity of backgrounds and experience of those in the field of facilitation, it is difficult to single out those characteristics that effective facilitators have in common. In general, though, an effective facilitator:

1. Is a person who has self-knowledge that is gained from a breadth and depth of personal experience. This knowledge cannot be gained from textbooks or formal education. It comes, rather, from working extensively with other people and from working through one's own personal values. A facilitator is likely to manifest these characteristics through behaviors such as:
   - Listening actively;
   - Being sensitive to team members' feelings;
   - Accepting people as they are;
   - Making space and time for working with others;
   - Avoiding personal crusades and dogmatic views;
   - Clarifying his or her personal values;
   - Confronting people and issues positively; and
   - Clarifying problems in a helpful way.

2. Has a foundation of practical theory. This does not mean an ability to regurgitate other people's theories, impressive though this may

seem. It does mean that the facilitator is able to draw on research and theory in a relevant way to guide his or her work.

3. Is open and realistic. Some facilitators will promise the world to their clients. Others are subtle manipulators who attempt to con or even threaten others into changing their behavior. An effective facilitator will be open in giving feedback to others and will be quite explicit about his or her own values. He or she also will develop a clear contract at the beginning of an assignment that will define the expectations and responsibilities of both client and facilitator.

4. Can work with the team on the here-and-now issues, but also can encourage the members to visualize ways of improving in the future. However, beware the facilitator who lives always in the future, especially where results are concerned.

5. Accurately presents "snapshots" of the team. Copious notes should be taken, often of direct quotations, on issues such as the principles of the team, the team's role in the organization, goal clarity and commitment, relationships and accountability, decision-making processes and communication, leadership style and rewards, openness and trust, cooperation and competition, and relationships with other teams.

Facilitation helps people in teams to change the ways in which they behave. No change will be permanent unless the team implements new ways of operating. Progress requires new ways of thinking, perceiving, and behaving. We define the facilitator's role as that of an active listener, supporter, catalyst, coach, confronter, devil's advocate, disciplinarian, guide, and action planner.

- *Active listener:* Sometimes the facilitator should simply listen. When team members are sharing beliefs, emotions, or personal views, the facilitator is well advised to consider psychologically withdrawing—"being there but not being there." The facilitator allows the conversation to ebb and flow and waits until it is time to intervene.

- *Supporter:* The support of the facilitator is important. Individuals need to be encouraged and given air time. The team will need emotional support, especially in times of difficulty. A group norm needs to be established that members support one another. Functional support also may be needed: venues for meetings found, notes written up, position papers written, and so on.

- *Catalyst:* The facilitator alters the ways in which the team behaves by paying attention to issues that the team usually fails to address. The facilitator acts as a catalyst to encourage a constructive and open climate marked by thorough and candid debates.

- **Coach:** As a facilitator works with many teams, he or she develops an understanding of how teams should operate. The facilitator then can act like the coach of a sports team, providing direction and encouragement. There is a second coaching role for the facilitator: working with the team's leader. Effective coaching can help the leader to adopt a constructive role in the team-building process.

- **Confronter:** The facilitator "holds up a mirror" so that the team can reflect on its performance. This is confronting, especially when interpersonal relationships are an important issue. The skills of giving effective feedback are vital. Whenever possible, the facilitator's feedback should be checked for accuracy against the perceptions of others. The most useful help is direct, open, and concrete commentary. Feedback is not judgmental or evaluative; instead, feedback describes the situation or the other person's behavior, thus allowing the receiver of the feedback to evaluate himself or herself.

- **Devil's advocate:** Teams develop a myopic way of seeing the world that prevents them from testing their arguments. Unfortunately, such distorted logic is always treacherous. The facilitator needs to be able to question, to generate informed debate, and to stimulate the thorough exploration of options—in effect, to act the part of devil's advocate. The facilitator must confront illusions of invulnerability, excessive and unwarranted optimism, discounted warnings, or declining ethical standards. Derision of other groups, censorship of divergent views, and ignored adverse information is particularly dangerous.

- **Disciplinarian:** Many experienced leaders prefer to deal with matters that are comfortable, urgent, or concrete. Team building often requires looking at issues that are uncomfortable, long-term, and abstract. In order for the team to tackle important underlying issues, the facilitator needs to set standards and adhere to them despite others' frustration, fatigue, or accusations of irrelevance.

- **Guide:** Many leaders of teams are ill-trained in the techniques of structured problem solving and decision making, for example, and thus are unaware of ways to improve the quality of their decisions. The facilitator must act as a guide—an educator, trainer, or demonstrator. The facilitator needs a "bag" of skills, techniques, and practical models.

- **Action planner:** Leaders seldom are efficient planners. Too often, resolutions are made but are never recorded or implemented. The facilitator must become the action planner for the team, noting actions, identifying responsibilities, and recording minutes. This role has an instructional function: the team observes effective planning in action and eventually learns to take over the function itself.

FINDING AN EFFECTIVE FACILITATOR

When an organization has no need for a facilitator, it may be bombarded with advertisements that promise dramatic consulting results in every conceivable field—from accounting to Zen meditation. Paradoxically, when the same organization needs a specific kind of consulting, finding the right facilitator can be a challenge. Sometimes it seems as though all the good facilitators have migrated to greener pastures, are booked until next year, or were last sighted heading for the desert to write a book.

With patience and persistence, an organization *can* find the right facilitator—in business schools, in other centers of management education, in large and small consulting firms, in other companies, or in independent practice. Facilitators hold many different titles, the most common being group facilitator, group-training specialist, and team-building consultant.

The best way to find the right consultant is to seek recommendations from people who have had good experiences with that consultant. To do this, check with companies or other organizations that have done some work in team building. A second approach is to ask a business school to recommend someone. If this fails to produce results, find a management publication in your field of interest; then contact the publisher or the author to ask whether he or she knows of any suitable consultants. If you still have no success, try the larger consulting firms that specialize in personal skills and group training or contact a management association. A word of warning: when approaching large institutions or consulting firms, remember that you will be working with one person, not the institution, so check on the person who will be doing the work.

CHOOSING A SUITABLE FACILITATOR

Before you engage the services of a facilitator, it is wise to check out his or her work, looking for relevance to your needs and level of quality. Facilitators should be pleased to refer you to past clients. Another tactic is to interview several facilitators and to select the candidate who best meets your needs. Discuss your problems with each facilitator and evaluate the strategy that is proposed. Does it feel right? Realistic? Not too slick? Not too vague?

Facilitators should demonstrate some of the behavioral skills that they will use in your team-building session. Reject facilitators like the one who disrupted an entire office with his pushy and pompous telephone manner. When the facilitator was connected with the manager and announced that he was a "specialist in human relations," the manager, having heard the effects of the man's behavior, said, "I don't believe you!" and hung up.

An important criterion in selecting a facilitator is whether any warmth, trust, or understanding develops between you and the facilitator. This is critical because a facilitator will be trusted with the confidences and the well-being of the team. The initial problem-exploration phase that the facilitator conducts with the leader and the team (before any commitment to that facilitator is made) should probe deeply enough to enable the team members to develop a sense of whether working with the prospective consultant would feel "right."

Before signing a contract with a consultant, make sure that he or she can devote sufficient time and energy to the needs of your team.

Finally, can you afford the consultant? Consulting services are not inexpensive, but a good consultant can make all the difference in the success and effectiveness of your team.

MANAGING YOUR FACILITATOR

Effective management of the facilitator will reduce the risk of a negative or unproductive team-building experience. Consider the following steps before and during your work with a facilitator.

1. Review and identify the group's needs. What issues and problems does the team identify? Can these be handled within the team or should they be addressed by someone in the larger organization? The Team-Review Survey can be of great use in answering these questions.

2. Have the team members reach consensus on the need (or lack thereof) for an external facilitator. If there is a general feeling that skilled outside help is necessary, proceed to step three.

3. Use the techniques outlined earlier to find several suitable facilitators and have them meet with the team members.

4. Select the most appropriate consultant for your needs.

5. Develop a contract for the consultant's services. This is not necessarily a formal, written document; often it consists of a mutual understanding about the following:

   • The initial diagnosis of the problems to be addressed;

   • The method(s) of addressing these problems;

   • How much further diagnosis is required and how it will be done;

- The relationship between the consultant and the team members (especially the leader);
- The role that the consultant prefers to hold;
- The design of the initial activities;
- The method(s) of progress review;
- The method(s) of measuring success;
- The schedule for the consultant's services;
- The time frame for the implementation of changes agreed on in team building;
- The amount of time required for the consultant to complete the team-building process; and
- The cost of the consultant and the method of payment.

6. Complete the initial diagnostic work and plan the initial activities. As much as possible, this should be performed by and agreed on by the entire team.
7. Start work. Review.
8. Identify how and approximately when the facilitator will begin to withdraw from the team. An effective facilitator's main goal is to help the team to become strong enough to handle its own development without regular external help. Make sure that this issue is raised with the facilitator before starting the team-building process.
9. After you have found a capable facilitator, it is both kind and helpful to value his or her services. It is not easy to be a facilitator, who is excluded from the emotional satisfaction of being part of a growing and developing team. As the team members become closer, the facilitator often feels a deep sense of isolation.

Part 2:

The
Team-Review
Survey

5

The Team-Review Survey

The effectiveness and well-being of any team must be assessed by the team itself. The foundations have been laid, benefits listed, caveats sounded, and processes explained. Now the time has come to delve and search—to focus on your team. To do this, the team members should complete the Team-Review Survey.

Before the team undertakes the Team-Review Survey, it is important to define which team is being assessed and to ensure that all those involved freely agree to complete the instrument as a team assignment.

The team's leader, who may or may not serve as the facilitator for the administration, scoring, and interpretation of the Team-Review Survey, should understand the purposes and objectives of the instrument before his or her team begins the process. After giving a precise definition of the team to be assessed, the team members will complete a 108-item instrument (a sample copy of the instrument begins on page 49) whose items are statements about the team's methods of functioning, the team members' impressions of one another and of their leader, and so on. The facilitator then will walk the respondents through the scoring process, the result of which is the identification of the three major "blockages" that impede the team's functioning.

The concepts of strengths and blockages are vital to an understanding of our approach to team building. Our approach was derived from our investigation of teams in industry, commerce, education, social welfare, shipping, media production, and military organizations. We tried to analyze the strengths and weaknesses of these work teams and to evaluate their levels of effectiveness. It became clear to us that teams are not built on production lines like pressed steel components; rather, if the environment is favorable, teams grow like crystals. It is helpful to think of team building as a series of steps toward maturity. As the team progresses toward maturity, it has to overcome problems. If these problems are not faced and resolved, they become what we call *blocks* or *blockages*.

Blocks inhibit the flow of team energy. Twelve distinct types of blocks can be identified, and each hampers team effectiveness in its own way.

When a block is fully cleared it enables positive energy to flow and, in a way, the block becomes a *generator* of energy. Each team has to find ways of overcoming its blocks and transforming them into generators. We define a fully developed team as one that possesses the twelve generators to a satisfactory degree.

A team's scores on the Team-Review Survey, therefore, provide invaluable information and the potential for future growth. After the data have been collected and identified, the remainder of the session is devoted to discussing them. Some groups find it helpful to work through each participant's responses separately and to discuss his or her responses to the key questions. Such a discussion can lead the team in many directions but should conclude with a summary of key points and a discussion of possibilities for future action.

At later meetings, all team members are asked to suggest activities that they think would be of benefit to the group. After an assessment of the best course to follow, a three-month action plan is developed. Review meetings are arranged, preferably at two-week intervals, and a team-development program is begun. After the team-building process has commenced, leaders should encourage team members to be a little adventurous and to enjoy themselves. Experiment with the materials while allowing time to discuss the results at the levels both of thinking and feeling.

Team effectiveness cannot be measured with scientific precision. Although the Team-Review Survey examines the key aspects of a team's effectiveness, much of the reported information clearly is subjective. Because of the obvious importance of the leader's own standards, it is necessary for the leader to examine his or her method of evaluating the effectiveness and maturity level of a team.

In the chapters that follow the instrument, we explain each generator and blockage in depth, as well as their relationship to the results of the Team-Review Survey. Each chapter begins with a list of the instrument questions that apply to the blockage and generator that is discussed in that chapter. Each chapter concludes with a list of suggested activities that will help the team to explore that chapter's particular blockage and transform it into a generator.[2]

AN EFFECTIVE TEAM

A team that is mature and effective is the result of painstaking effort. Problems have been worked through, relationships have deepened, and

---

[2] A complete index to the activities is found on pages 167-172.

roles have been clarified. Successful teams share several attributes and demonstrate significant achievement in the following areas:

1. Appropriate leadership. The leader has the skills and desire to develop a team approach and allocates time to team-building activities. Management of the team is seen as a shared function. Team members other than the leader are given the opportunity to exercise leadership when their skills are appropriate to the needs of the team.

2. Suitable membership. Team members are individually qualified and contribute to the mix of skills and characteristics that provide an appropriate balance.

3. Commitment to the team. Team members are committed to the aims and purposes of the team. They are willing to devote personal energy to building the team and to supporting their fellow team members. Even when they work outside the team boundaries, the members feel that they belong to and represent the team.

4. Constructive climate. The team's climate encourages people to feel relaxed, able to be direct and open, and prepared to take risks.

5. Desire to achieve. The team is clear about its objectives, which are believed to be worthwhile. It sets targets of performance that require members to "stretch" but that are achievable. Energy is devoted primarily to the achievement of results, and team performance is reviewed frequently so that members can find ways to improve.

6. Clear corporate role. The team contributes to corporate planning and has a distinct and productive role within the greater organization.

7. Effective work methods. The team has developed lively, systematic, and effective ways of solving problems.

8. Role clarity. Roles are clearly defined, communication patterns are well developed, and administrative procedures support the team approach.

9. Critique without rancor. Team and individual errors and weaknesses are examined without personal attack to enable the members to learn from experience.

10. Well-developed individuals. The latent potential of team members is fulfilled by their membership in the team. They become more outgoing and capable, and their professional competence is enhanced as they meet new challenges with one another's support.

11. Creative strength. The team generates new ideas from the interactions of its members. Some innovative risk taking is rewarded, and the team will support new ideas both from its members and from the outside. Good ideas are put into action.

12. Positive intergroup relations. Relationships with other teams are developed systematically to maintain contact with others and to identify opportunities for collaboration. There are systems of regular contact and of reviews of joint or collective priorities. Team members are encouraged to work with members of other teams.

The sample copies of *The Team-Review Survey* and the accompanying facilitator's instructions that appear on the following pages are for the reader's reference; a copy of each item is included with each order.

THE TEAM-REVIEW SURVEY[3]

Instructions

Part 1:

In the box, write a clear, complete description of the team to be reviewed. You may write either the names of all team members or a clear and accurate description of the team.

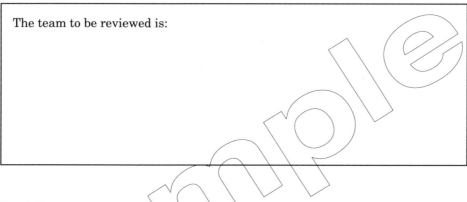

The team to be reviewed is:

Part 2:

For each of the following 108 statements, think about the statement in relation to the team that is being surveyed. There may be times when you find it difficult to answer a particular question, but do the best that you can. It might be useful for later discussion to note in the margins the numbers of questions that you find particularly difficult to answer.

Keep in mind that the accuracy of this survey depends on your openness and honesty in answering the questions. This is not a test with "right" and "wrong" answers; rather, it is a tool for promoting thought and discussion.

Use the following scoring system:

If the statement is *generally true* for this team, write "A" in the blank next to the question number.

If the statement is *sometimes true* for this team, write "B" in the blank next to the question number.

If the statement is *generally untrue* for this team, leave that item blank.

Put an asterisk (*) next to the numbers of statements that you find especially significant or difficult to answer. These statements will be explored later.

---

[3] Copies of *The Team-Review Survey* are available from the Pfeiffer & Company office from which this book was purchased. A copy of the Facilitator's Instructions for Administering the Team-Review Survey, printed on sturdy paper, is included with each order of instruments.

A = *Generally true* for this team
B = *Sometimes true* for this team
Blank = *Generally untrue* for this team

_____ 1. The leader and team members spend little time in clarifying what they expect and need from one another.

_____ 2. The quality of the team's work would improve if team members upgraded their technical qualifications.

_____ 3. Some of the team members feel that the aims of the team are hardly worthwhile.

_____ 4. People in this team sometimes do not say what they really feel.

_____ 5. The objectives of our team are not clear.

_____ 6. Team members are unsure about the team's contribution to the larger organization.

_____ 7. We do not achieve much progress in team meetings.

_____ 8. The objectives of some team members conflict with those of others.

_____ 9. When team members are criticized, they feel that they have lost face.

_____ 10. No real effort is spent on developing each member of the team.

_____ 11. Not many new ideas are generated by the team.

_____ 12. Conflicts between our team and other groups are quite common.

_____ 13. The leader rarely tolerates leadership efforts by other team members.

_____ 14. Some team members may be unable to handle the current requirements of their work.

_____ 15. Team members are not really committed to the success of the team.

_____ 16. Team members sometimes put down others in the team.

_____ 17. The team rarely achieves its objectives.

_____ 18. Our team's contribution is not clearly understood by other parts of the organization.

_____ 19. During our team meetings, we do not listen to one another.

_____ 20. Members of the team do not fully understand one another's roles.

_____ 21. Members restrain their critical remarks to avoid rocking the boat.

_____ 22. The potential of some team members is not being developed.

_____ 23. Team members are wary about suggesting new ideas.

A = *Generally true* for this team
B = *Sometimes true* for this team
Blank = *Generally untrue* for this team

_____ 24. Our team does not have constructive relationships with some of the other teams within the organization.

_____ 25. The leader gives his or her views before other members of the team have contributed their views.

_____ 26. Our mix of skills is inappropriate for the work that we are doing.

_____ 27. I do not feel a strong sense of belonging to this team.

_____ 28. It would be helpful if the team could have "clear-the-air" sessions more often.

_____ 29. In practice, low levels of achievement are accepted.

_____ 30. If the team were disbanded, the organization would not feel the loss.

_____ 31. Team meetings lack a methodical approach.

_____ 32. There is no regular review of each team member's objectives and priorities.

_____ 33. The team is poor at learning from its mistakes.

_____ 34. Team members do not keep up to date.

_____ 35. This team does not have a reputation for being innovative.

_____ 36. The team does not respond sufficiently to the needs of other teams in the organization.

_____ 37. The leader does not welcome feedback about how the team sees his or her performance.

_____ 38. People outside the team consider us unqualified to meet our work requirements.

_____ 39. I am not prepared to really put myself out for the team.

_____ 40. Important issues are swept under the carpet and not worked through.

_____ 41. People are given few incentives to stretch themselves.

_____ 42. There is confusion between the work of this team and the work of other teams in the organization.

_____ 43. Team members do not prepare carefully for meetings.

_____ 44. Team members are uncertain about their individual roles in relation to the team.

_____ 45. Attempts to review events critically are seen as negative.

A = *Generally true* for this team
B = *Sometimes true* for this team
Blank = *Generally untrue* for this team

_____ 46. Little time and effort are spent on individual development and training.

_____ 47. This team seldom is innovative.

_____ 48. We do not actively seek to develop our working relationships with other teams.

_____ 49. The leader is not willing to have his or her ideas challenged.

_____ 50. The team's total level of ability is too low.

_____ 51. There are cliques (subgroups) within the team.

_____ 52. Team members are expected to conform.

_____ 53. Energy is absorbed in unproductive ways and is not put into getting results.

_____ 54. The role of our team is not clearly identified within the organization.

_____ 55. The team does not have an effective means for making decisions in meetings.

_____ 56. Some team members' roles overlap.

_____ 57. We would benefit from an impartial assessment of how we work.

_____ 58. Team members have been trained only in their technical disciplines.

_____ 59. Good ideas seem to get lost.

_____ 60. Significant mistakes could be avoided if we had better communication with other teams.

_____ 61. The leader makes decisions without talking them over with the team members.

_____ 62. We need an infusion of new knowledge and skills to make our team complete.

_____ 63. I do not feel proud of being a member of this team.

_____ 64. Differences of opinion among team members are not worked through properly.

_____ 65. Team members have different views as to what success is.

_____ 66. We do not have an adequate way of establishing our team's objectives and strategies.

_____ 67. We seem to get bogged down when a problem is being discussed in team meetings.

A = *Generally true* for this team
B = *Sometimes true* for this team
Blank = *Generally untrue* for this team

_____ 68. I could not, with complete confidence, define my own role within the team.

_____ 69. We lack the skills to review our effectiveness constructively.

_____ 70. The team does not take steps to develop its members' skills.

_____ 71. New ideas from outside the team are not accepted.

_____ 72. In this organization, teams and departments tend to compete rather than to collaborate.

_____ 73. The leader does not adapt his or her style to changing circumstances.

_____ 74. The team needs the stimulus of more radical or creative people.

_____ 75. Team members are not striving to make this a winning team.

_____ 76. Members of this team do not really care for one another as people.

_____ 77. We seem more concerned with keeping up appearances than with achieving results.

_____ 78. The organization does not utilize the vision and skills that this team has to offer.

_____ 79. We have team meetings but do not properly examine their purposes.

_____ 80. Important work does not get done because no one is responsible for it.

_____ 81. Performance would improve if constructive criticism were encouraged.

_____ 82. People who are quiet or uncertain are overridden.

_____ 83. It would be fair to say that the team has little vision.

_____ 84. Other teams/departments have a low opinion of us.

_____ 85. The leader does not adapt his or her style to the needs of each team member.

_____ 86. Team members do not adapt to the changing needs of the team.

_____ 87. If a team member gets into difficulty, he or she usually is left to cope with the situation alone.

_____ 88. The team lacks a sense of energy and excitement.

_____ 89. Nothing that we do could be described as excellent.

A = *Generally true* **for this team**
B = *Sometimes true* **for this team**
Blank = *Generally untrue* **for this team**

_____ 90. The team's objectives have not been related systematically to the objectives of the whole organization.

_____ 91. Decisions that are made at meetings are not recorded properly.

_____ 92. Team members could collaborate much more if they would work through their own responsibilities to other team members.

_____ 93. Little time is spent on reviewing what the team does, how it works, and how to improve it.

_____ 94. Team members are not encouraged to take on new challenges.

_____ 95. Only a few members suggest new ideas.

_____ 96. We do not get to know the people who work in other teams in the organization.

_____ 97. I do not know whether our team is adequately represented at higher levels of the organization.

_____ 98. The team lacks a blend of different but complementary personalities.

_____ 99. Team members are committed to individual goals at the expense of those of the team.

_____ 100. I believe that team members do not really trust one another.

_____ 101. We often fail to finish things in a satisfactory manner.

_____ 102. Members of this team would not be able to define exactly what value the team adds to the competitive advantage or excellence of the organization.

_____ 103. Our meetings do not resolve all of the issues that should be addressed.

_____ 104. Team members fail to resolve role conflicts among themselves.

_____ 105. We do not learn from our mistakes.

_____ 106. Team members are not encouraged to go outside the team to broaden their knowledge and skills.

_____ 107. Creative ideas often are not followed up with definite action.

_____ 108. If we worked better with other teams in the organization, it would help us all to be more effective.

TEAM-REVIEW SURVEY SCORING SHEET

The grid below has 108 cells, each of which is numbered to correspond to a statement in the Team-Review Survey. Transfer your responses from the survey items to the corresponding cells in the grid. Note that the grid is numbered in rows from left to right and from top to bottom.

1	2	3	4	5	6	7	8	9	10	11	12
13	14	15	16	17	18	19	20	21	22	23	24
25	26	27	28	29	30	31	32	33	34	35	36
37	38	39	40	41	42	43	44	45	46	47	48
49	50	51	52	53	54	55	56	57	58	59	60
61	62	63	64	65	66	67	68	69	70	71	72
73	74	75	76	77	78	79	80	81	82	83	84
85	86	87	88	89	90	91	92	93	94	95	96
97	98	99	100	101	102	103	104	105	106	107	108
												Total number of A's
												Total number of B's
I	II	III	IV	V	VI	VII	VIII	IX	X	XI	XII

TEAM-REVIEW SURVEY INTERPRETATION SHEET

After you have totaled all of the A's and B's for each of the twelve columns in the answer grid, transfer your totals to the corresponding Roman numerals on the chart below. Multiply each "A" score by 3, but count each "B" score as 1. Compute your personal total score for each of the twelve categories.

Working with your team members, add the members' total scores and divide by the number of team members who completed the Team-Review Survey to calculate the team's average score for each category. Enter each average score in the corresponding box.

Next, rank your team's average scores. The category with the highest average score will be ranked 1; the category with the second-highest average score will be ranked 2; and so on. Transfer your team's rankings to the answer grid.

	Your "A" Score (x 3)	Your "B" Score (x 1)	Your Total	Your Ranking	Team Average	Team Ranking
I. Inappropriate Leadership						
II. Unqualified Membership						
III. Insufficient Group Commitment						
IV. Unconstructive Climate						
V. Low Achievement Orientation						
VI. Undeveloped Corporate Role						
VII. Ineffective Work Methods						
VIII. Lack of Role Clarity						
IX. Soft Critiquing						
X. Stunted Individual Development						
XI. Lack of Creative Capacity						
XII. Negative Intergroup Relations						

In the spaces provided below, list the categories in which you received your three highest-average scores and in which your team received its three highest-average scores. Your team's three highest-scoring categories are its primary blockages.

Your Highest-Average Scores   **Names of Blockages**

1. _____   _____

2. _____   _____

3. _____   _____

Team's Highest-Average Scores   **Names of Blockages**

1. _____   _____

2. _____   _____

3. _____   _____

Diagnosis

After you have listed the blockages for which you and your team received the highest scores, your team may choose the blockages that it wishes to address in team building. (The blockages that the team selects may be, but do not have to be, the ones in which it received the highest scores.) Brief descriptions of the twelve blockages appear on the next page. When your team has chosen its topics for further work, please complete the statement in the box below.

Based on a review of the twelve blockages, our team chooses to address the following issues:

Summary of the Twelve Team Blockages

1. *Inappropriate leadership:* The team leader is unable and/or unwilling to use a team approach and does not encourage the use of team-building activities. He or she often uses a "command" decision style rather than a "consensus" decision style. The leader does not share his or her power or leadership responsibilities.

2. *Unqualified membership:* Team members are not qualified (professionally or socially) to contribute to the team and thus do not help it to achieve its goals.

3. *Insufficient group commitment:* Team members are not committed to the aims and purposes of the team and are reluctant to expend personal energy on meeting the team's goals.

4. *Unconstructive climate:* The team's climate discourages members from feeling comfortable, from being direct and open, and from taking risks.

5. *Low achievement orientation:* The team may not understand its objectives; and if it does, it may not believe that they are worthwhile. It may set targets that are either uninspiring or unreachable. Team members' performance may be reviewed only infrequently.

6. *Undeveloped corporate role:* The team is excluded from corporate planning. It may not understand its role within the greater organization.

7. *Ineffective work methods:* Problems that are faced by the team are not solved effectively and efficiently.

8. *Lack of role clarity:* Team members' roles are not clearly defined, efficient communication procedures have not been developed, and administrative procedures are not supportive of the team's efforts.

9. *Soft critiquing:* In order not to upset team members, neither group nor individual errors and weaknesses are addressed directly and thoroughly enough so that they are eliminated.

10. *Stunted individual development:* Team members have not developed the maturity and confidence needed to be assertive or to deal with other members' strong personalities.

11. *Lack of creative capacity:* Team members do not generate new ideas, perhaps because risk taking is not encouraged and rewarded by the organizational climate.

12. *Negative intergroup relations:* Teams that are required to work together compete rather than collaborate. Because teams do not meet to compare agendas, their priorities may conflict.

FACILITATOR'S INSTRUCTIONS FOR ADMINISTERING THE TEAM-REVIEW SURVEY

Goals

I. To help team members to explore the strengths and weaknesses of their team.

II. To determine whether the team members have the desire and the energy to begin a team-building program.

III. To help team members to define and understand the characteristics of effective teamwork.

Time Required

A minimum of two hours.

Materials

I. One copy of the Team-Review Survey for each team member.

II. A pencil and blank paper for each team member.

III. A newsprint flip chart and a felt-tipped marker.

IV. Masking tape for posting newsprint.

Physical Setting

A quiet room with chairs and tables in which team members can sit and write comfortably.

Process

I. One person acts as the team's facilitator. He or she may be a professional facilitator, or the team's leader may undertake the role. It is important that the facilitator review the process in depth prior to the session. He or she should take at least one hour before the meeting to become familiar with the Team-Review Survey, its goals, and its interpretation. The facilitator then will act as coordinator and discussion leader for the session.

II. The facilitator gives a brief explanation of the process that the team is about to undertake. He or she emphasizes that voluntary involvement is essential and invites team members to express any concerns that they may have. Only if there is full agreement should the Team-Review Survey be distributed and the activity continue. (Ten minutes.)

III. The facilitator distributes the Team-Review Survey, pencils, and paper. The team members are asked to complete the Team-Review Survey, jotting down the numbers of any items to which it is particularly difficult to respond. (Twenty minutes.)

IV. The team members are instructed in the scoring of their completed instruments using the grid provided on the Team-Review Survey Scoring Sheet. (Ten minutes.)

V. Using the Team-Review Survey Interpretation Sheet, the facilitator guides the team members in charting their reactions. The facilitator explains the framework of analysis to the team member. Team members may wish to compare and contrast one another's scores immediately after they complete the survey or, if it was completed prior to the meeting, at an early stage in the session. The following procedure quickly brings out key points and provides a reliable bank of reference information.

1. The facilitator determines whether each team member is willing to share his or her scores. The team members should be allowed to decide whether scores will be collected anonymously or each member will announce his or her scores. After a method has been agreed on, the facilitator lists the scores on a flip chart and totals the scores for each category. (The team's total scores for each category should be listed on one sheet of newsprint so that the members can compare the totals for ranking purposes.)

2. The facilitator explains that individual variations in scores may be due to differences in criteria that were used in completing the survey or to differences in respondents' perceptions. In either event, variations in scores are significant and warrant discussion.

3. The team members are told that the team's average scores and rankings are of special significance because they reveal both the team's areas of strength and its perceived weaknesses and needs for development. Low scores indicate areas of strength that probably require only reinforcement; high scores indicate probable blockage areas that require attention.

4. The facilitator states that the team-ranking column on the interpretation sheet will help the team to identify its significant blockages. The ranking of priority 1 is assigned to the blockage that received the highest total team score; the ranking of priority 2 is assigned to the blockage that received the second-highest total team score; and so on until the team has ranked the blockage with the lowest total score, which is designated priority 12. After determining the blockage rankings, the facilitator draws the participants' attention to priorities 1, 2, and 3. These are the areas in which the team is weakest and that will require the most clarification and action in the future.

(Fifteen minutes.)

VI. The facilitator begins a discussion of the results, and the team members discuss the following questions for approximately twenty minutes each.

1. How important are the Team-Review Survey results to this team? Do you think that they portray this team accurately?

2. Which of the team's strengths and weaknesses are significant? Do they correspond to the team's rankings?

3. What resources are we prepared to devote to strengthening the team and to working through the team's blockages? How many blockages are we prepared to address?

The facilitator should make sure that the participants respond in specifics to question 3. For example, one way of measuring the team's commitment is to allocate money to the team-building project. If a team is willing to spend scarce resources on development, then it is clearly committed; and action is more likely to follow.

(At least one hour.)

VII. After the discussion has been concluded, the facilitator has the team decide whether to proceed with team building; consensus must be reached. Sometimes it is useful to allow the team members a few days for reflection before making a final decision. If the team wishes to proceed with team building, it can move through the steps outlined in *Improving Work Groups,* which will help it to experiment, to adapt, and to learn from its experiences.

Part 3:

Team Development

6

Effective
Team Leadership

SURVEY ITEMS

1. The leader and team members spend little time in clarifying what they expect and need from one another.

13. The leader rarely tolerates leadership efforts by other team members.

25. The leader gives his or her views before other members of the team have contributed their views.

37. The leader does not welcome feedback about how the team sees his or her performance.

49. The leader is not willing to have his or her ideas challenged.

61. The leader makes decisions without talking them over with the team members.

73. The leader does not adapt his or her style to changing circumstances.

85. The leader does not adapt his or her style to the needs of each team member.

97. I do not know whether our team is adequately represented at higher levels of the organization.

The most important factor in determining the quality of a team's work is the way in which its leader operates. Leadership, like virtue, is hard to identify; and, paradoxically, it is most clearly recognized in its absence. A leader who is unwilling to use a team approach, or who lacks the skills to develop a team-based style of management, will squash any team-building initiative.

Not all team leaders approach the task of team building in the same way. There are nine principal styles of team leadership.[4] The nine styles are:

The Value-Driven Style

This leader has deeply held beliefs about what is good and bad, important and unimportant. By expressing these values, he or she captures others' interest and good will. The value-driven leader is persuasive in his or her conviction and invokes others' respect and admiration. This type of leader excels at clarifying values, making effective presentations, delving beneath the surface, and getting to the heart of the matter. This leader attracts others by appealing to their moral sense.

The Goal-Setting Style

The goal-setting leader ensures that his or her aims and objectives are understood clearly by all concerned. His or her efforts are directed toward achievement; subordinates' performance is monitored, goals are set, and coordinated plans are provided. By establishing milestones and avoiding being put off the scent, he or she influences situations. This leader's style is administrative in the best sense of the word. He or she uses management techniques to channel others' efforts. The goal-setting leader's skills include objective setting, action planning, assessing performance, and controlling and giving feedback. This leader drives others by obtaining their commitment to objectives, then keeping their performance on track.

The Need-Fulfilling Style

This leader is helpful in a practical way. He or she identifies others' needs and shows how they can be fulfilled. The leader's usefulness as a problem-solving resource is the source of his or her credibility and influence. The need-fulfilling leader is sensitive, an active listener, client centered, an action planner, and a cooperative counselor. This type of leader attracts others by winning their confidence and by being a valued colleague.

The Visioning Style

This leader's visions of the future, in which there are better ways of doing things and in which wrongs are righted, give others meaning and direction and a sense of possibility. In addition to his or her ability to express vivid

---

[4] This analysis is developed from an activity in *50 Activities for Unblocking Organizational Communication* (Vol. 2) by Dave Francis. Aldershot, U.K.: Gower, 1991. Used with permission.

images, the visioning leader is imaginative, optimistic, far-sighted, and practical. He or she is an architect of the future. This leader attracts others by providing them with a positive direction.

The Rational-Persuasive Style

This leader is persuasive in argument and debate. Facts are valid. He or she collects data, evaluates information, builds a logical case, and presents sound arguments. The rational-persuasive leader appeals to others' reason and intellect, and his or her position is defensible and reasonable. This leader's strengths are analysis, concept development, logical thought, and formal presentation. He or she attracts others through argument and rationality.

The Pushing/Driving Style

This leader is influential because he or she uses "weight" to cajole, demand, insist, or push people to act in a desired fashion. He or she has a forceful, controlling, and dominating style, although these traits may be expressed in subtle ways. The pushing/driving leader is prepared to make a fuss to achieve his or her objectives. This leader knows how to work with people, is assertive, and uses conflict constructively. He or she influences others with personal will power.

The Institutional Style

This leader's formal authority is his or her basis of power. He or she obtains influential positions and builds a role in the organization. The institutional leader seeks the authority to allocate resources to further preferred causes. He or she concentrates on laying the foundations for projects. The institutional leader excels at organizational design, planning, performance control, and administration.

All but the very smallest organizations have hierarchies—people who are in charge of other people. Managers are accountable to their bosses for the behavior and performance of the subordinates who report to them. Some functions of leadership, such as answering on behalf of the group and regulating output, are firmly tied to the managerial role. Although the power that is inherent in a managerial position may be used only rarely, it is ever-present and permanent. Thus, the institutional leader drives others with legitimate power.

The Educating Style

This leader exposes people to new ideas, experiences, concepts, and possibilities, and acts as a teacher, educator, catalyst, counselor, and guide to enrich others' experience by opening their minds. He or she causes people to discover that their current thinking or behavior is in some way inadequate. The educating leader excels at diagnosing others' strengths and weaknesses, designing learning, communicating principles, and teaching. He or she attracts people by inspiring them to reevaluate the world around them.

The Supportive Style

The supportive leader encourages and empowers people to identify their needs, to evaluate their options, to formulate action plans, and to take the initiative. He or she has a positive attitude, adds extra energy, and gives others confidence and moral support. The supportive leader does not guide or manage others; rather, he or she enables others to act. This leader's skills include listening, counseling, giving positive feedback, and advising. An effective supportive leader is skilled at balancing people's feelings and the team's process. He or she motivates others by giving them energy.

The nine styles of team leadership provide a useful framework for team leaders to use in assessing their own approaches to leadership. It is important for leaders to remember that the ability to act in a range of styles skillfully is the real test of their abilities.

SITUATIONAL LEADERSHIP®

Some of the most valuable theories of leadership were developed by Paul Hersey and Ken Blanchard (1982), who determined that there should be a correlation between the leader's style of leadership and the group's level of development ("maturity"). The leader must assess the team members' level of willingness and abilities in relation to each task. This notion is in keeping with the nine styles of leadership that were outlined previously.

Each leadership style is based on a set of assumptions and beliefs about the nature of leadership; these are explored in more detail below.

PHILOSOPHIES OF LEADERSHIP

Those who have traveled in the Far East will recognize that Western concepts of leadership are not embraced universally. Particularly interesting is the ancient concept of Yin and Yang, the two forces that many Chinese people believe shape the universe. The idea that Yin and Yang represent the principles of male and female is an oversimplification. Yin is a holding force, directed toward the earth; while Yang is a moving force, directed toward the heavens. Both need to exist in harmonious opposition. The paradox that reality requires opposing forces is well understood by the Chinese. This notion has profound implications for leaders. In essence, the leader's role is Yin, which has been called the female force; the leader needs to hold the members of the team together. Opposites should be encouraged rather than discouraged; if differences of opinion do not occur, the team is ailing. Each force within the team needs an opposite: concern with output needs to be balanced by concern for team spirit, conservatism needs to balance radicalism, and so on. The role of the leader becomes that of a holding force that finds harmony in diversity. Ideally, the leader constantly should seek out opposites for his or her team. Balanced direction only emerges from conflict.

Another set of powerful ideas about leadership comes from Japan, wherein the Samurai tradition still underpins much management theory. The Samurais were warriors who learned to strengthen their will power until it was stronger than life itself. For example, a Samurai would go into battle feeling that he had already lost his life. Therefore, he was unafraid; the worst had already happened. The idea that will power can be strengthened is not well understood by many Westerners. Yet will power, the ability and willingness to go through thick and thin for one's beliefs, is the primary source of respect from others. Today's leaders need and want respect for their beliefs and convictions; however, seeking to gain respect for its own sake is counterproductive.

LEADERSHIP IN ORGANIZATIONS

The principle of hierarchy is reflected in the language that is used to describe team roles. Words such as *supervisor* and *subordinate* convey the message. Even though it is easy to assume that managers have a "divine right" to exercise their authority, such an assumption is alien to true team building. Clearly, leaders do have special responsibilities and functions, but if they want to use a team approach, it is important for them to avoid hiding behind the symbols of eminence and the mannerisms of distance.

A leader's development of an open approach with his or her team is an interesting process with wide intellectual appeal. However, it often becomes uncomfortable—perhaps frightening—and many team members shy away from it. In team building, one duty of the team leader is to make this developmental process happen. The leader can do this by setting an example of openness, by demonstrating an open approach, and by giving others opportunities to lead the team. Team members are much more concerned with their leaders' *actions* than with their words. Therefore, personal exposure and willingness to deal with uncomfortable issues are necessary requirements for the leader. After the barriers have been broken, the release of energy and greater depth of relationships among team members more than compensates for the period of discomfort.

It is important to note that not all leaders of teams hold the official title of manager. Well-developed teams that know the strengths of their members rearrange their hierarchies to suit the tasks at hand. Hence, it is quite possible for the leadership of a team to be diffuse, with different people acting as leader at different times. This productive and effective process can be blocked by an "official" team manager who refuses to distribute information and relinquish control. Paradoxically, a manager often can be of most service to his or her team by letting go of the organization-given right to decide and execute and by encouraging the people who are best equipped to lead at the time.

LEADERSHIP SKILLS

A person who is taking the leadership role in a team must:

- Be deeply aware of the impact of his or her leadership style on the team members;
- Know and respect deeply the power of teamwork;
- Be authentic—trustworthy and honest;
- Be affirmative, expressing an optimistic yet realistic view of human nature;
- Desire to empower and utilize the resources of others;
- Have a wide range of leadership styles available;
- Show deep commitment to all members of the team;
- Bring clarity to objectives;
- Believe in the possibility of continuous improvement;
- Build a climate that is both supportive and confronting;
- Ensure that work methods are satisfying and effective;
- Maintain a discipline within which relevant issues are explored; and
- Strongly attack all impediments to effectiveness.

These functions are very different from the conventional managerial roles of making decisions, exerting control, and exercising discipline. The chief difference is that a team-oriented manager perceives decisions, control, and discipline as team functions rather than as his or her sole prerogative. In today's organizations, with their emphasis on team centeredness, many people feel stifled by "traditional" managers. People tend to describe managers who have turned them off and sent them looking for other jobs as overbearing, inconsistent, malicious, unenergetic, stultifying, and game playing.

One of the most difficult—yet most important—tasks for the leader is to question rigorously the everyday practices of the team. Leaders need to develop their awareness and perceptual abilities.

SUGGESTED ACTIVITIES

2. Leadership-Functions Analysis
3. Leadership-Style Profile

REFERENCE

Hersey, P., & Blanchard, K. (1982). *Management of organizational behavior: Utilizing human resources* (4th ed.). Englewood Cliffs, NJ: Prentice-Hall.

7

Choosing the Members of a Team

SURVEY ITEMS

2. The quality of the team's work would improve if team members upgraded their technical qualifications.

14. Some team members may be unable to handle the current requirements of their work.

26. Our mix of skills is inappropriate for the work that we are doing.

38. People outside the team consider us unqualified to meet our work requirements.

50. The team's total level of ability is too low.

62. We need an infusion of new knowledge and skills to make our team complete.

74. The team needs the stimulus of more radical or creative people.

86. Team members do not adapt to the changing needs of the team.

98. The team lacks a blend of different but complementary personalities.

People tend to shine only in certain areas of endeavor, because of different talents or inclinations. Likewise, people are imperfect in different ways. One may be excessively disciplined, another may be too wild, and a third may have an extremely narrow range of knowledge or expertise. In a team, one person's weakness can be counterbalanced by another's strength. Therefore, teams have a range of resources that is impossible for one person working alone to acquire.

The concept of balanced team construction can be studied from two distinct but complementary perspectives: team members' technical capabilities and individual members' roles.

TEAM MEMBERS' TECHNICAL CAPABILITIES

A team must be suited to its purpose. The capabilities of team members must match the tasks that they are undertaking. Imagine a research team whose task is to trace the origins of the universe to the first seconds after the "big bang." The team members probably would be world-class scientists skilled in quantum mechanics, theoretical physics, computer modeling, and so on. A team composed of a heart surgeon, a stand-up comedian, and an airline pilot could not begin to work on the task, no matter how brilliant they were. The point is that the appropriate range of technical capabilities must be present or accessible to the team.

This is difficult to achieve in practice. Traditionally, those responsible for recruitment and selection have focused on people as individuals rather than as potential team members. In today's team-centered organizations, however, this policy is questionable. At the most basic level, academic or technical qualifications should be identified and used as criteria in the selection of personnel. A person's role as a team member—as a piece of the team "jigsaw puzzle"—is equally important as that person's individual attributes. New team members ideally should complement and add to the team's range of technical competence. For example, consider a gang of master criminals who intend to steal a famous diamond. The following experts are included in the gang:

- A boss to train the team for the assignment and to manage the team.
- A planner to analyze situations, propose tactics, and communicate plans to the other members.
- A lookout to provide real-time data on the activities of the forces of law.
- A heavy (or two) to carry equipment and deal with interruptions.
- A safe cracker to gain entry to the safe or vault.
- A driver to expedite the gang's departure.

The gang may not need one person for each function because some people may be able to perform several roles. Nevertheless, the gang as a whole must comprise the right mix of abilities, and it will be more likely to succeed in its mission if each member knows the challenges and difficulties that the others face as they perform their specialized roles.

Builders of teams owe many of their ideas and theories to sociology and to the total quality management (TQM) movement, which emphasizes that it is vital to understand the function of a team by answering the question, "What should the team be contributing to its customers?" Notice that the question is worded "what should" instead of "what does." This word choice is deliberate and reflects the leader's desire to create a team to fulfill a vision, not just to maintain the status quo.

The following example illustrates this point. A top team is running a strategic business unit (SBU) in a large corporation. The functions of the team include tracking changes in the marketplace, understanding competitors' behaviors, forming strategies, establishing performance ratios, and providing coherent leadership for the entire business unit. The top SBU team needs people with the skills to fulfill all of these functions.

Over time, a team's functions almost always change. Consider teams of operators in a motor-assembly plant. Twenty years ago, most of the work was routine and monotonous, as people did the work. Now, however, robots perform almost all routine assembly operations; and team members function not as assembly-line workers but as troubleshooters, analysts, and multiskilled fitters. The evolution of team functions happens even in unlikely settings; for example, the tasks of a Roman Catholic priest are significantly different today than they were a generation ago. The implication for the team builder is clear: the specification of the team's existing and desired functions is an essential step in determining the skills and expertise that team members must possess.

Technical and professional skills also can become obsolete. Continuous learning and development are essential for people at all levels within the organization. This has been recognized as essential for upper management for many years, but the principle applies to people at all levels in organizations. Through the power of the Japanese philosophy of *kaizen* (continuous improvement), it has become clear that all employees need to be involved in the continuous processes of learning and innovating. Without kaizen, there is a slow decline in team effectiveness because new concepts, methods, and applications are being developed in almost all fields. Keeping one's technical qualifications up to date and relevant requires more than a passing acquaintance with innovation. New ways of thinking should be understood in depth.

When team members' technical capabilities are specialized, the role of team building is to build bridges of understanding between team members. It is vital that all team members understand and respect one another's contributions. In fact, in the early stages of the team-building effort, much time needs to be spent on clarifying each member's specialties and skills, including those of part-time members. Of course, capabilities are only part of the analysis; personal interests and motivations also are important. In general, we do better those things that we want to do. One of the advantages of teamwork is that it enables people to perform more frequently the activities that they enjoy.

Different team-membership profiles are needed for different types of teams and for teams at different stages of development. A team that harvests and processes sugar cane needs different competencies than does the group that markets the thousands of tons of sugar world wide.

TEAM MEMBERS' ROLES AS INDIVIDUALS

At the Henley Management College in England, an industrial psychologist, Dr. Meredith Belbin (1982) conducted several highly significant experiments. His subjects were participants in a lengthy management course who were formed into teams to complete a management game as part of their program. Belbin, using a range of psychometric tests, studied the personalities and mental capabilities of team members and discovered that each person had a strong tendency to play a distinct but limited set of roles from definable categories. The brilliance of Belbin's work was that he identified and described eight basic team roles that provided the basis for later research. After much research, Belbin found that he could predict, with a surprising degree of accuracy, the performance of each team merely by analyzing the results of a battery of psychometric tests conducted for each member. The winning teams were those whose membership was broad enough so that all necessary roles were filled. Belbin also learned how to introduce a new member with much-needed skills into a failing team, thus greatly increasing the chances of its success.

Unfortunately, Belbin's work was undertaken with teams that neither had been exposed to the benefits of team building nor had learned how to employ a structured approach to problem solving and decision making. However, research by one of the authors has concentrated on developing a more comprehensive set of team roles; these are summarized below.

The Process Manager (PM)

The process manager channels human resources to get things done. This person forms teams, identifies people's strengths, sets objectives, structures meetings, clarifies issues, allocates roles, and maintains momentum. The process manager studies members of the team to determine their individual strengths and weaknesses and maintains an analytical and observant approach. He or she brings organization and structure to the team and ensures that goals and terms of reference are clear. The process manager is able to draw out the best from people and has the skills of a good chairperson. He or she tends to be controlled, self-confident, calm, and skilled as a listener and communicator.

All leaders are required to play this role on occasion, and the relevant process-management skills can be learned through training and practice.

•❖ *Key contribution:* Ability to chair meetings

The Concept Developer (CD)

The concept developer ensures that ideas are developed and evaluated and serves as the team's entrepreneur. He or she builds on ideas, tests their validity, visualizes the potential impacts of different courses of action, sees possibilities, and transforms ideas into practical proposals. The main strength of the concept developer is the ability to see the potential benefits of an idea. He or she will often "play" with novel proposals to assess their worth. This role has been described as that of an "intellectual opportunist." When someone suggests an idea, the concept developer will elaborate on it so that it can be evaluated.

The concept developer is imaginative, responsive, and ingenious. He or she excels at design and development but has the tendency to move too quickly from idea to idea. The CD is able to see the potential of an idea, to evaluate alternatives, and to visualize the idea's impact. However, the true concept developer has relatively little interest in actual implementation, preferring to move onto the next problem. To be of maximum effectiveness in a team, the CD must stay with an issue long enough to hand it off with sufficient information to the team members who will implement his or her idea. The concept developer thrives on complex problems and enjoys a challenge. The key skills that he or she brings to the team are vision; imagination; ingenuity; precise, logical thinking; and understanding.

•❖ *Key contribution:* Vision

The Radical (RA)

The radical contributes unexpected perspectives by considering problems from unusual perspectives, by envisioning new possibilities, by adopting unconventional approaches, by generating insights, and by producing novel proposals. Radicals take a fresh look at situations. They refuse to accept traditional wisdom, which can be perceived as abrasive or irritating by other members of the team. The radical may be described as the maverick of the group. He or she is unfettered by conventional wisdom and prefers to think things through independently. The true radical is a free spirit.

Radicals often have a strong sense of intuition. Research suggests that the right side of the brain (which supposedly is nonlinear and more creative) is particularly active in radical thinking. The radical's ideas may not always be well-presented or fully formed, but they usually are innovative and unusual. Radicals' presentations always contain an element of the unexpected. Radicals often score highly on tests of mental ability, and they welcome complex problems or novel challenges. The radical excels at generalizing, classifying, adducing evidence, and simplifying.

•❖ *Key contribution:* Conceptualizing

The Harmonizer (HA)

The harmonizer builds morale by being relationship oriented; he or she is caring, supportive, encouraging, understanding, sociable, and good at resolving conflicts. The harmonizer believes that efficiency is based on good relationships. By building and maintaining morale, the harmonizer creates an atmosphere that is ripe for commitment, cooperation, and good performance. The person who plays the harmonizing role pays attention to others and strives for order. He or she often is idealistically motivated.

The harmonizer wants people to get along. He or she works hard to create and sustain a constructive atmosphere. The harmonizer is unusually sensitive to others' feelings and is a keen observer. If someone is feeling demotivated or upset, the harmonizer will know. Although the harmonizer is supportive and encouraging, he or she should not be allowed to become weak or indulgent. The harmonizer tries to ensure that team members enjoy one another's company and that they value their membership in the team.

•❖ *Key contribution:* Supporting

The Technical Expert (TE)

The technical expert contributes information and expertise and possesses a specialized and valuable body of knowledge acquired through extensive training and experience. He or she may be a finance director, marketing director, corporate planner, personnel director, etc. This team member may remain silent until an issue that is relevant to his or her field of specialty is raised. Technical experts are partisan, but their advice may be most important. Only the expert may know enough to give an informed opinion.

•❖ *Key contribution:* Specialized know-how

The Output Driver (OD)

The output driver ensures that jobs get done, which requires setting targets, meeting objectives, and completing tasks. Performance is valued for its own sake. The OD has a strong commitment to quality and integrity, as well as a strong sense of duty that is based on personal standards. The output driver pushes to get things done and checks to ensure that standards are upheld. Organizing resources is a way of life for this person. People who play the output-driver role are inclined to be somewhat anxious and worried about deadlines. The output driver may be intolerant of error, somewhat inflexible, and autocratic. These are the people who are always checking to see whether things could go wrong at the last moment. Their strengths lie in creativity in tactics and contingency planning. Output drivers often are described as conscientious.

•❖ *Key contribution:* Pushing

The Critic (CR)

The critic brings to the team objective observations and carefully weighed opinions to assist in decision making. He or she stands back, makes judgments, considers possibilities, looks for pitfalls, sounds notes of caution, questions proposals, and challenges ideas. The critic is neither negative or positive; rather, he or she is objective.

The critic takes a mental step back from the team, exercises caution, and avoids getting caught up in the enthusiasm of the moment. He or she tends to be conservative, judging new proposals against past precedents. The critic's role is an important antidote to "groupthink"—the dangerous, collective hypnotism that teams sometimes experience. He or she hunts for possible pitfalls before agreeing to a course of action and is willing to play "devil's advocate." Critics may appear to be the least enthusiastic members of the group and may be accused of being cold. However, an able and experienced critic's wisdom is invaluable to a team. Critics are skeptical, decisive, accurate, and stable but somewhat distant contributors.

•❖ *Key contribution:* Impartial evaluation

The Cooperator (CO)

The cooperator is a diligent observer who actively assists the team in whatever ways are needed. He or she fills gaps by helping, by cooperating, by being prepared to work hard, and by being adaptable. The true cooperator is a jack of all trades and is willing to do whatever is necessary to be useful. Cooperators will organize resources and tackle mundane or unpleasant jobs without complaint. Cooperators may lack assertion skills and may become excessively helpful (i.e., take the role of victim). They are quick to see blockages to progress. The role of cooperator requires excellent observation skills, generosity, enthusiasm, lack of concern for protocol, and a broad range of ability.

•❖ *Key contribution:* Flexibility

The Politician (PO)

The politician shapes the team's collective viewpoint with his or her opinions, results orientation, influence, ability to build alliances and to guide others, persuasiveness, and consciousness of power. The politician acts like a magnet to pull people in the same direction. He or she knows the right thing to do and deliberately tries to influence others in that direction. This is a person who will lobby, persuade, deal, and influence. Such people often are notably tenacious and persistent, bouncing back after setbacks. They are continually working on the best ways of implementing ideas.

The role of the politician has been described as that of a "shaper," for the politician molds and shapes opinions and objectives. Politicians have a strong sense of personal values and are high in autonomy; they feel that they are masters of their own lives. They often are high strung, outgoing, dynamic, and intolerant. Politicians are quick to react, to move the team toward action, and to identify personally with success.

➡ *Key contribution:* Drive

The Promoter (PR)

The promoter links the team to others by being outgoing, sociable, and relationship oriented; by investigating resources; and by feeling out ideas and possibilities. Promoters are "fixers" and enable things to get done. The promoter deliberately gathers useful contacts and makes connections outside the team. This role suits extroverted people who make friends easily. The promoter is a salesperson on behalf of the team and sometimes acts as a bridge.

This role is particularly important in upper-management teams, as there is a need to link the organization to the community, to industry bodies, to key customers, and to related organizations and suppliers. In such cases, the promoter acts as the figurehead of the organization. However, the promoter can be something of a gadabout, moving from one situation to another and never seeing things through. Promoters are tolerant, socially adept, outspoken, nurturing, and cooperative.

➡ *Key contribution:* Linking

SPECIALIZATION

One question that naturally follows the previous discussion of roles and specialties is, "Should team members try to be jacks of all trades, or should each member focus on that in which he or she excels?" To use a musical analogy, the question becomes "Should a musician learn every instrument in the orchestra, or should he or she specialize in one or two?" Today we understand that specialization often is the most effective way to utilize a person's talents; it is better to focus on a limited set of objectives than to try to do everything and to end up performing at a mediocre level. This analysis is significant to the team builder for two reasons.

First, part of the basic rationale for teamwork lies in the recognition that people are fundamentally different. Teams are organizations that combine people with dissimilar talents to create an entity that is more than the sum of its parts. Second, teams need to have an inner symmetry. Each person's contribution should balance the contributions of others. Furthermore, the nature of the members' talents must serve the task in hand. Still, teams need an inner coherence and harmony. It therefore follows that one of the primary tasks of the team's leader is to construct a team that is (as much as possible within the existing constraints) suited to its purpose. To do this, the leader must think not just about individual members' talents and skills but about the team as a single entity.

SUGGESTED ACTIVITIES

4. Team-Roles Analysis Questionnaire
5. Use Us—We're the Best

REFERENCE

Belbin, M. (1982). *Management teams: Why they succeed or fail.* London: Heinemann.

Commitment

SURVEY ITEMS

3. Some of the members feel that the aims of the team are hardly worthwhile.
15. Team members are not really committed to the success of the team.
27. I do not feel a strong sense of belonging to the team.
39. I am not prepared to really put myself out for the team.
51. There are cliques (subgroups) within the team.
63. I do not feel proud to be a member of this team.
75. Team members are not striving to make this a winning team.
87. If a team member gets into difficulty, he or she usually is left to cope with the situation alone.
99. Team members are committed to individual goals at the expense of those of the team.

Teams will not flourish if their members lack a sense of duty, obligation, and responsibility. All teams require commitment from their members. This means that team members must give their energy, attention, and time to support the development of the team. If they do not, the team will be nothing more than a loose assembly of individuals. Team membership involves an element of personal sacrifice, because each team member gives up a degree of autonomy and abandons single-minded, self-interested pursuits. For example, some members view their teams as political forums for achieving the best for themselves at the expense of others. This attitude is always destructive.

Some teams become fragmented by partial commitment, which often is referred to as "cliqueness." In any group, certain people will naturally be drawn to one another and will form natural alliances. "It's chemistry" is the usual expression. Most interpersonal alliances are not displayed obviously; rather, they are subtle undercurrents that are felt rather than measured. These alliances, which result in some people's looking to others for support, can become potent negative forces in the team. Interestingly, those who are excluded from such alliances often feel a sense of emotional outrage, as they perceive themselves as victims of prejudice. People in groups typically take the roles of "persecutor," "victim," or "rescuer." Interpersonal interactions, when observed with these insights, hold much new meaning.

Commitment fuels a team's energies and aspirations. In a team setting, commitment means that the team members decide that the team will not fail due to their lack of initiative or motivation. This provides the energy to overcome setbacks. Commitment to the team welds the members into a close and interdependent unit. Commitment can be developed only in a climate of fairness. "Fairness" has been insightfully described (Sashkin & Williams, 1992) as trust, consistency, truthfulness, integrity, expectations, equity, influence, justice, and respect. Without fairness, a team nurtures a seed of decay.

Commitment is not a once-and-for-all decision. A couple can come together, vow their lifelong dedication to each other, then change their minds and steer their marriage along a mutually destructive path. Similarly, team members can change their minds and withdraw their support. In an effort to make sure that this does not happen, the team's leader needs to find ways for the team members to renew their commitment to the team's objectives.

DEVELOPMENT OF COMMITMENT

People become committed to teams for one or more of the following nine reasons:

1. **Self-interest:** The person believes that he or she will gain a personal advantage by being a member of the team.
2. **Belief in a vision:** The person believes that he or she is helping a greater vision come to fruition.
3. **Belief in the leader:** The person feels loyal to the leader of the team.
4. **Common values:** The person shares the team's set of basic beliefs about what is and is not important.
5. **Mutual support:** The person feels a sense of comradeship with his or her colleagues.
6. **Sense of duty:** The person is committed because he or she believes that this is part of the price to be paid for being in the team.
7. **Demanding tasks:** The person is committed because he or she wants to achieve goals or a standard of accomplishment that requires the assistance of others.

8. *Feeling of accomplishment:* The person is committed to the the team because, working together, the members participate in a shared celebration of success.

9. *Structured socialization:* New people are welcomed and made to feel part of the team.

It can be helpful and revealing for team members to ask themselves, "How did I become committed to teams in the recent past?" In fact, as part of the research for the second edition of this book, we asked a number of managers to answer this question. One respondent replied as follows:

> I suppose the most important thing was the way that Mary Lou (the team manager) went out of her way to explain to me why the team's work was important. She told me about what had happened in the past few months and why I was important. When I met the others, they really welcomed me; I felt at home from the very beginning. It seems like a small thing, but someone had taken the trouble to program my name into the electronic-mail system so that when I turned my computer on, it said "Welcome to the team, Pete." On the second evening, all the members of the team had arranged an evening session at the local bar. It was all very informal, but we talked about our backgrounds and got to know one another. And Mary Lou saw to it that I presented a summary of my initial impressions of the team at my first weekly communication session. By the end of the third day, I found myself saying "we" when I was talking about the team.

This person's thoughts provide some important insights into the nature of commitment. New members need to be introduced, welcomed, valued, and given the opportunity to encounter the other members of the team (this is called "structured socialization").

The growth of commitment is an indication of the stage of maturity of the team. As the team develops, the level of commitment will grow. At the highest level of team commitment, such as that displayed by soldiers in battle, team members will put the welfare of the group above their own safety.

One test of team commitment is to assess the level of the members' enjoyment of one another. Team members who are close have fun together. Members turn to one another for counsel, conversation, and support. A mature team will pour its resources into helping a team member who is having difficulties. When a member leaves the team, it is a significant event and is marked in a notable way. Committed team members value one another's contributions and express their feelings openly. They identify positive contributions from others and express their gratitude. Each person feels appreciated. As a result, team members feel liked, appreciated, and encouraged to express their creativity and energy.

There is a downside to such closeness: commitment to the team often clouds members' objectivity in decision making. The psychology is subtle:

as team members become closer, they support one another's positions in conflicts—perhaps whether or not their colleagues are in the right. It is easy to see how blind commitment could undermine the quality of a team's work. Unquestioned mutual support could lead a team to tolerate inadequate performance or to protect some members from objective evaluation. In the long run, this behavior is harmful to a team because marginal members cannot be "carried" without the team's effectiveness being weakened. It is important to recognize that commitment needs to be directed toward the team's performance as well as toward the other team members.

TWO METHODS OF INCREASING TEAM COMMITMENT

Shared Team Goals

Shared goals are present when all members have participated in a process that clarifies the team's collective goals. All members need to believe that the team's goals are both achievable and important. If the team's expressed goals seem to be impossible to achieve, team members will become cynical and demotivated. Frustration and disillusionment are the consequences of a team's failing to ensure that action follows insight.

Shared team goals define the following:

- Basic beliefs and values;
- The behavior that is desired from each member;
- The ways in which the team culture should be developed;
- The outputs that are needed;
- The team's roles within the larger organization;
- Key success factors—what the team has to do really well; and
- What the team will always strive to do and what it will never do.

Teams need to establish goals or objectives so that every member clearly understands what should be achieved. Broad goals must be narrowed into specific objectives. Objective-setting systems should not destroy creativity by being excessively rigid. All team members need to know their performance targets and to think about how they will meet them. Finally, they need to understand how their performances will be evaluated.

Personal Warmth

Personal warmth is likely to be expressed in such phrases as "It's great to have Don aboard" and "It feels good to work here." Mature teams demonstrate respect and understanding for their members that are built on mutual understanding and tolerance. Members are willing to give and receive honest personal feedback because they are confident that the feedback is intended to be supportive and helpful.

Commitment can be developed consciously by teams that deliberately set aside time for commitment-building activities. We think it is important that these activities become "routine maintenance" in organizations—part of "the way we do things around here."

SUGGESTED ACTIVITIES

6. Team-Development Stages
7. Designing a Team-Building Workshop

REFERENCE

Sashkin, M., & Williams, R.L. (1992, Autumn). Does fairness make a difference? *Organizational Dynamics.*

Positive Climate

SURVEY ITEMS

4. People in this team sometimes do not say what they really feel.
16. Team members sometimes put down others in the team.
28. It would be helpful if the team could have "clear-the-air" sessions more often.
40. Important issues are swept under the carpet and not worked through.
52. Team members are expected to conform.
64. Differences of opinion among team members are not worked through properly.
76. Members of this team do not really care for one another as people.
88. The team lacks a sense of energy and excitement.
100. I believe that team members do not really trust one another.

As a team develops, informal rules (norms) that influence the members' behavior quickly become established. The precise guidelines under which the team operates rarely are written down but are understood by its members. After a while, these rules become habitual and are communicated (by a process that sociologists call *socialization*) to new team members. The combination of traditions, habits, relationships, practices, rules, beliefs, and attitudes that characterize a group is called its *climate*. Much of the responsibility for establishing a group's climate belongs to the team's leader.

Ask a group of people to think of a highly successful team and to identify the three key characteristics that made it great. Without fail, the answers will include statements such as "People were open with one another," "I felt tremendously valued in this group," "There was a real buzz of excitement when we were together," and "I enjoyed myself enormously." All of these statements relate to that hard-to-define aspect of teamwork that we call climate. The following example emphasizes the nature and importance of a positive climate and illustrates what can happen when a climate turns negative.

One of the authors of this book had close friends whose home was a haven of sheer delight. It overlooked the ocean and seemed to glow with happiness. Then the husband, began to find other women irresistibly attractive and to spend more and more time away "on business." The family's home life outwardly appeared the same, but subtle changes began to take place. No longer was there that effortless spontaneity or whole-hearted openness. The children, who (as all children do) served as barometers of the emotional climate, began to fret and whine. The interactions between husband and wife became planned dramas rather than easy conversations. Eventually the wife found an incriminating hotel receipt and confronted the husband, who admitted his transgression (but not all the dalliances) and said that he would mend his ways. Three months later a woman phoned the wife and said, "I think you should know that your husband is in love with me." The wife listened, believed what she heard, and the essential fabric of the marriage was destroyed in three minutes.

Just as in a marriage, certain conditions must exist in order for a positive team climate to form. The following conditions must be present:

- **Trust:** The belief that deeds will follow words and that the other person will take your interests into account. High-quality relationships cannot operate where there is deceit.
- **Openness:** People say what they really think and feel.
- **Authenticity:** No interpersonal games are played.
- **Closeness:** Team members feel affection for one another, and a similar, basic set of moral values draws team members together.
- **High energy:** The team has a strong positive atmosphere and zest for life.

TRUST

Trust is an enabling force. It is the foundation of a positive climate, providing stability during turbulence and change. There are five conditions that must be met in building a climate of trust.

The first criterion is *honesty*—telling the truth even when the truth is embarrassing, unpalatable, or shocking. People accept that they cannot expect to know everything at once, but when information is conveyed, it must be the truth.

The second criterion is *consistency*. A person who wavers on matters of principle is soon distrusted, even though he or she may be telling the truth in each individual moment. A trustworthy person must have a core of stability, consistency, and dependability.

The third criterion is *realism*. People whose statements are incredible or fanciful are not believed, even though they may be totally sincere. Naïve people, too, are not trusted, even though they may trust themselves.

The fourth criterion is *application*. Deeds must follow words. A person who promises to do something must follow through or else his or her credibility will be destroyed. This is especially important when promises are made about rewards or punishments. If a person is offered something positive (e.g., a promotion, a bonus, or an incentive) that fails to materialize, the offerer immediately will lose credibility. The same principle holds true when a disciplinary action is threatened but not carried out.

The fifth criterion is *compassion*—a belief that others (especially those with power) will act fairly and decently. We trust people who appear to have our best interests at heart, and we want to be treated with compassion and dignity.

OPENNESS

Not all group climates support the development of a team approach. Team building requires a climate of openness—one in which problems, concerns, and feelings are aired. A climate of openness must exist in order for team members to establish relationships that are genuine and close.

Openness is not easily achieved or maintained. Too many people have learned to hide feelings and thoughts that they think are unacceptable. However, it is vital in team building that members take risks and suggest initiatives. It should be possible for people to be wrong without being made to look foolish. An executive at NASA expressed the idea brilliantly when he said, "We do not punish error; we only punish the suppression of error."

The degree of openness in a team affects its climate so profoundly that it is helpful to identify the advantages and disadvantages of an open approach. The main advantages of an open approach are:

- Frustration is reduced.
- Closer personal relationships are established.
- Problems are clarified and can be addressed.
- Feedback is given, enabling others to learn and develop.
- Energy is released as issues become unblocked.

However, there are also potential drawbacks to group openness:

- People may feel more vulnerable.
- People's lack of certainty is exposed and may be interpreted as weakness.

- Others may feel threatened by openness and may react by becoming hostile.

- Problems that are difficult to handle are brought into the open and thus must be faced.

AUTHENTICITY

In recent years, our knowledge of interpersonal interactions has been augmented by the theories of transactional analysis (TA), which describe psychological transactions and strategies based on the "games" that people play to achieve their ulterior motives.[5] Psychological games between people take place as part of a struggle for control or comfort. They reflect a person's need to reinforce his or her theory of life, no matter how destructive this might be. In a sense, then, such games are part of the psychic underground of the team and almost invariably are damaging to the fostering of an open climate.

The following negative transactions (games), which are described briefly in the terminology of TA, apply to both men and women "players." The games that are named here are merely a sampling; many more varieties exist.

Kick Me. Some people set themselves up for psychological punishment, for example, by failing to complete an assigned task. The self-styled victim gets a smart "kick" and goes away to lick his or her wounds, thereby feeling justified in maintaining a negative view of life.

If It Weren't For You. Failure is rationalized as being caused not by the person but by forces outside the person (i.e., by forces not under his or her control). Consequently, the player does not feel responsible because he or she has been treated "unfairly."

Yes, But.... This is a superiority strategy or "ego trip" whereby a person appears reasonable but is, in fact, not receptive to others' suggestions. It most typically is played by people who agree to others' suggestions or ideas (implying an open and receptive mind set) and then say "but...," thus discounting the other people's ideas.

Blemish. This game often is played by people who set out to destroy a suggestion or report by criticizing a minor blemish (such as grammar or punctuation), thus ignoring the suggestion's merits. The blemisher psycho-

---

[5] For a further discussion of transactional analysis, the reader is referred to *Born to Win* by Muriel James and Dorothy Jongeward, Reading, MA: Addison-Wesley, 1985.

logically destroys the work on the basis of its often-insignificant faults. By faulting others, the blemisher makes himself or herself feel important.

I've Got So Much To Do. In this game, the player takes on mountains of work, spends every waking hour desperately trying to catch up, and finally "proves" his or her inability to cope. The "payoffs" for this player are feelings of depression and of being unable to contribute. This feeling of honest defeat can give this player a comfortable position of self-justified isolation.

I Lead a Frugal Life, So.... This strategy of superiority stems from the unspoken attitude of "I don't waste things, nor am I extravagant, so I'm more honorable than you." This use of humbleness is a way of putting distance between the player and others and is another isolationist tactic.

There Is No Way Out, So What Can You Do? After evaluating all options, this player decides that each possible choice has drawbacks. So, the "logical" thing to do is just to sit back and let things go because "after all, there is nothing worthwhile to aim for, is there?"

Let Me Help You. This game player's payoff stems from feeling more charitable, sensitive, and self-denying than others. Sometimes there is a vicious competition to see which player is the most self-effacing.

I've Got a Wooden Leg, So What Can You Expect of Me? This player blames his or her failures on a particular characteristic (such as race, accent, background, or weight) as if to say, "With my handicap no one can expect me to do well." Again, this is a way for a person to feel justified through failure.

Now I've Got You, You Son of a Bitch. By finding excuses to make others suffer, some people satisfy a need in themselves. Dedicated players of this game often will demonstrate superhuman patience and skill in waiting for potential victims to make mistakes; they may even manipulate the victims into doing so. Then they pounce. "After all," this game player seems to say, "if I can make someone suffer, then I must be important."

Although games underlie many of the interactions between people, effective teams place a value on authentic relationships and try to purge games from their interactions.

CLOSENESS

Closeness can be defined as a feeling that another is known and is important. Teamwork requires that members establish a climate in which members care for one another but, as a work team is neither chosen nor a family group, the required level of closeness is less than is required for other personal relationships.

Closeness is not without its difficulties, which were demonstrated by Professor Janus as follows: "The more amiability and esprit de corps among the members of a policy making in-group, the greater is the danger that independent critical thinking will be replaced by groupthink, which is likely to result in irrational and dehumanizing actions directed against out groups" (Janus, 1972). Janus suggests the deliberate encouragement of free speech as an antidote to groupthink. He advocates, for example, that "one or more outside experts or qualified colleagues within the organization who are not core members should be invited to each meeting on a staggered basis and should be encouraged to challenge the views of the core members" (Janus, 1972).

Closeness affects the ways in which people perceive the world around them. We pay attention to those who we feel are part of our "inner circle" and tend to ignore those who are not. In studying a new team, it is possible to detect many indications of the lack of concern among various team members; this will undermine the team's work until closeness is fostered.

Closeness among team members is built on:

- *Shared experience:* Each member has been through emotionally significant experiences with the others;
- *Disclosure:* People say what they really think and feel;
- *Respect:* Each team member respects the other members' unique qualities and characteristics;
- *Shared goals:* The team members share similar purposes;
- *Gratitude:* People say that they value the input of others and act accordingly; and
- *Shared values:* A similar, basic, common morality draws the team members together.

A team's capacity to deal with interpersonal problems is a good test of its level of closeness. A close team practices effective interpersonal problem solving, which combines both confrontation and respect for individual opinions. Effective listening skills are particularly helpful. When a disagreement or communication breakdown occurs between members, the team members work at identifying the source of the problem. For example: Is there actually no problem between John and Bob? Is the problem just an illusion? Does only John have a problem? Only Bob? Both? Are there basic differences in John's and Bob's beliefs and values that might preclude any possible reconciliation? It often is worthwhile to clarify the different sides of an interpersonal issue by using one's own viewpoint as a starting point.

The steps in this encounter may be examined through the following key questions:

- What kind of relationship do I want to have with this person after this conflict has passed?
- What specific behaviors that the other person exhibits present problems for me?
- What effects do the other person's behavior have on me?
- What changes in the other person's behavior would I like to see?
- Can I state the problem clearly and share my feelings without confusing or blaming the other person?
- If the other person becomes defensive or aggressive, do I practice effective listening?
- How effectively can I use systematic problem-solving approaches to deal with difficult situations?
- Do I and the person with whom I have a conflict negotiate "space" for ourselves so that conflicts of values have minimum impact?

HIGH ENERGY

The most satisfied teams are those in which every member feels enlivened by his or her participation. High energy is self-perpetuating because the team members become accustomed to operating in that fashion and feel compelled to give their all to the team. An attitude of "we can do it" is adopted. Setbacks are recognized but are not allowed to demoralize team members. The team is an exciting place to be. Much of this comes from the personal qualities of the team's leader. The following leader behaviors or attitudes help to generate high energy in a team:

- *Recognition of success:* The leader honors achievements both great and small.
- *Sense of winning:* The leader communicates the feeling that participation in the team is participation with winners.
- *Real challenge:* The leader knows and states that success will not come easily.
- *Sharing of blockages:* The leader identifies and resolves potential difficulties early.
- *Payoff for members:* The leader helps each member to feel that he or she has gained something of real importance through participation.

The following key questions are based on many of the important issues that need to be considered when one is considering the effectiveness of a team's climate.

Group Climate

1. Are members encouraged and supported?
2. Are members' contributions valued and accepted?
3. Are all members brought into discussions and allowed to be heard?
4. Does the group set high standards in establishing procedures and in evaluating decisions?
5. Are personal issues dealt with compassionately? Do members fully accept the group's decisions?

Avoidance of Destructive Behavior

1. Do members withdraw from the group by daydreaming, by whispering to others, or by wandering from the subject?
2. Does any group member compete with others by attempting to offer the most ideas, to play the most roles, or to talk the most?
3. Do members act aggressively, criticize or blame others, show hostility, or deflate others?
4. Do members use the group for self-confession by delving excessively into personal, nongroup-oriented feelings or issues?
5. Do members disrupt the work of the group by clowning or by acting flippant?
6. Do any members argue for their own special interests or lobby unfairly?
7. Do any members block the group's progress by going off on tangents, by arguing too much about a belabored point, or by rejecting ideas without having given them due consideration?

SUGGESTED ACTIVITIES

8. Team-Climate Questionnaire
9. Fong Construction: A Study in Teamwork

REFERENCE

Janus, I.L. (1972). *Victims of groupthink: A psychological study of foreign policy decisions and fiascos.* Boston, MA: Houghton Mifflin.

10

Team Achievement

SURVEY ITEMS

5. The objectives of our team are not clear.
17. The team rarely achieves its objectives.
29. In practice, low levels of achievement are accepted.
41. People are given few incentives to stretch themselves.
53. Energy is absorbed in unproductive ways and is not put into getting results.
65. Team members have different views as to what success is.
77. We seem more concerned about keeping up appearances than with achieving results.
89. Nothing that we do could be described as excellent.
101. We often fail to finish things in a satisfactory manner.

One of the most significant experiments in team effectiveness took place in the 1930s. At Western Electric's Hawthorne plant, a group of behavioral-science researchers under the leadership of Elton Mayo (Roethlisberger & Dickson, 1936) observed groups of workers linking electrical connectors in their Bank Wiring Room study. They discovered that the workers' output was almost unaffected by the incentive system or by the blandishments of the supervisors. Workers believed that they should limit their productivity to maintain a steady work flow and to avoid some of their members' being declared "surplus to requirements"—a phenomenon that the researchers labeled "restriction of production." The workers did just enough to satisfy their bosses. The study revealed to the researchers the critical importance of high achievement norms to team development.

ACHIEVEMENT NORMS

A norm is a convention, habit, or standard. Consider how people keep their houses. Some people live in pristine cleanliness with "a place for everything and everything in its place," while other people create an unkempt and cluttered environment. After a while, either state becomes normal and unconsidered—a norm for that household. Team norms are established by three major influences: leaders ("opinion leaders"), the patterns that have been accumulated over the team's history, and the needs of team members.

Opinion leaders are the most significant forces that shape team norms. In almost every group there is someone whose opinion shapes the collective mind of the team. He or she is respected, admired, and influential. An opinion leader may or may not be the team's formal supervisor. Interestingly, much attention is now being paid to developing supervisors so that they learn to be effective opinion leaders, because achievement almost always slips when the leader becomes an inconsequential force in setting team norms.

The patterns that have been accumulated over the team's history also shape achievement norms—a phenomenon that is illustrated by the following case history. The authors studied a company that manufactured electric motors. For many years the company had specialized in winding intricate coils and had a strong production norm—output was king. So important was its commitment to performance that it tended to neglect new power-supply technologies. More innovative companies entered the market, but this organization continued to use the old methods in its manufacturing. The company eventually closed down. The accumulated patterns of the organization's history, which affected all of the operating teams, shaped the firm's destiny.

The needs of team members are the third element in establishing achievement norms. Clearly, the workers in the Bank Wiring Room study believed that collective job security was more important than high wages. They acted to ensure that their collective belief was more likely to prevail, no matter what management desired. There was a common need, which the opinion leaders (who were not, of course, the supervisors) in the bank wiring room voiced. Each person's beliefs, attitudes, and motives affected the group's achievement norms.

SETTING HIGH ACHIEVEMENT NORMS

Effective teams set positive group norms that lead to high standards of achievement. They review their use of resources with attention to their return on investment. Their main question is "Does our work actually produce results?" Because organizational teams exist to achieve tangible results, it makes sense to evaluate them on their ability to "deliver the goods." A work team that meets its members' needs for social contact but fails to meet the bottom-line requirements is not a successful one. Much can be learned from the behavior of a team of NASA engineers who discovered that the lunar-landing module that they had constructed was too heavy. They rigorously examined each component and made a piece-by-piece evaluation, reviewing the benefits of all units and simplifying them at every stage. They pared down each unit to its simplest and lightest form. This kind of vigorous review of benefits against drawbacks is a powerful method of increasing a team's effectiveness.

Each team member has personal standards, but individual standards can be modified considerably by group pressure. Accordingly, it is important to work as a team to define standards (norms) so that performance levels are set above the acceptable level, thus ensuring that the team constantly will strive to achieve excellence. It follows, then, that achievement should be valued and rewarded within the team. These rewards do not have to be financial, although material rewards certainly are relevant and welcome. High achievers are rewarded with a sense of personal significance and potency. An increased involvement in decision making and communication are rewards in themselves. In addition, high achievers have the opportunity to "stretch" and to learn new skills.

Because almost all endeavors fall prey to setbacks or plateaus at some point, a team should be able to handle both the practical aspects of setbacks and the emotional side effects. The team must be resilient and innovative in order to press on despite difficulties.

ACHIEVING OBJECTIVES

For a team to achieve a goal, the goal objectives must be shared by team members. An objective is a clear statement of what could and should be. Objectives must have a compelling quality. They are measures of a team's vitality; they focus the team's energy and provide tools for directing and integrating members' efforts. Together, a team's objectives become a statement of its collective intent and vision. The objectives need to be deeply held by all of the people who can help to transform the team's vision into reality. Objectives help in setting priorities and schedules and in allocating resources.

Generating clear and shared objectives requires skill. The team leader's task is to ensure that the team members have a clear and understandable outline of what needs to be achieved. It is helpful for the leader to review objectives regularly to determine whether they are still valid. Team objectives should be two-way: each member needs to gain something as the team achieves its goals.

Objectives may vary in their degree of specificity. Some objectives are expressed in very broad terms: "to provide an efficient city police force." Other objectives are extremely specific: "to wheel-clamp fifteen cars in Police Division J within the next hour." There also may be intermediate objectives, such as "to enable traffic to move through the city at an average speed of fifteen miles per hour for twenty-three hours per day."

Broad objectives are concerned with the "big picture." They liberate the imagination and clarify intent. Broad objectives sometimes are called *superordinate goals*—they relate to basic values and missions. Superordinate goals have a moral and uplifting quality. They can be spelled out explicitly. For example, Thomas Watson, Sr., designed IBM's corporate credo with three cornerstones: respect for the individual, customer service, and excellence in everything. Each team in IBM is charged with applying these superordinate goals in its own area.

In its "H-P way," Hewlett-Packard has defined the following superordinate goals:

- *Belief in people* (freedom);
- *Respect and dignity* (individual self-esteem);
- *Management by objectives,* rather than by direction (decentralization); and
- *A chance to learn by making mistakes.*

Such goals rise above profit targets by relating the goals and policies of the firm to deeper human needs and principles. As in IBM, each team at Hewlett-Packard is responsible for applying the organization's superordinate goals to its own areas. Superordinate goals, therefore, act as the DNA of the team; they are the building blocks from which the team is constructed.

High-achieving teams set two different types of objectives: *performance* and *competence* objectives. Performance objectives define what should be achieved in measurable terms. Competence objectives are qualitative and are set by asking the question, "What do we need to be good at in order to achieve our performance objectives?" Competence objectives tell the team what to emphasize; they focus the team's collective energy on what strengths need to be created. Output and competence objectives go hand in hand; they support each other.

In some situations the team's objectives may be indistinct. For example, a senior health-management team may be considering closing a small, local, geriatric hospital and moving the patients into a large medical facility.

Arguments both for and against this action exist. The patients will receive more professional care, but there are risks involved in disturbing long-established patterns. In addition, there are responsibilities toward relatives and friends to think about. Add to these the views of patients, the activities of local groups, the lack of community-care workers, government policies, the views of the local newspaper, and the cost implications; and it becomes difficult to determine the best course of action.

Several objectives may be pursued by a team at the same time. Teams should seek to identify all objectives and to reduce overlap or conflict. Teams also need to clarify and validate their objectives with other teams in that organization.

It is one thing to set objectives and quite another to put them into practice. When a team fails to meet its objectives, it needs to explore the process and to resolve its feelings of failure before morale erodes. The techniques of critiquing (discussed in Chapter 14) can help turn failures and setbacks into opportunities for development.

FUNCTIONAL ACHIEVEMENT

Obviously, teams strive to achieve different objectives. The top team at IBM corporate headquarters has very different objectives from those of an IBM sales team that is selling the latest hardware in Saudi Arabia. An approach to sociological analysis called *functionalism* provides useful tools for the team builder. Different teams fulfill different functions, depending on their positions within the larger organization. Teams need to be developed to meet specific functional requirements and to achieve their functional goals. Using Mintzberg's (1983) definitions, we can develop five categories of teams, each of which is suited to the achievement of different types of functional requirements.

Strategic-Apex Teams

At the top of the organization there are teams that set core strategies, determine major policies, and make key resource-allocation decisions. These are the strategic-apex teams, often called executive committees or boards of directors. A strategic-apex team strives to deliver the following:

- Carefully designed strategies and policies;
- A coherent vision for the organization;
- Strong leadership for the organization;
- Prudent resource-allocation policies;

- Effective relationships between the organization and the outside world; and
- Success in major deals.

Operating-Core Teams

At the core of the organization there are teams that carry out the basic work of the organization: cooking meals, teaching students, driving trains, and so on. These are the operating-core teams. These teams need to deliver the following:

- Necessary inputs;
- Transformation of inputs into outputs;
- Maintenance of systems and equipment,
- Distribution of outputs;
- Sales of outputs; and
- Continuous development of improved methods.

Middle-Line Teams

In the middle of the organization there are management teams that are responsible for the day-to-day control and coordination of the organization. These are the middle-line management teams. These teams need to deliver the following:

- Translation of strategies into operational objectives and tasks;
- Direct supervision of all employees;
- Effective communication both upward and downward;
- Close integration with other functions;
- Diagnosis and treatment of weaknesses; and
- Expert "how-to" guidance.

Technostructure Teams

Most organizations have expert teams that serve a research-and-development function—researching technologies, developing systems, and introducing change. These are the technostructure teams. These teams need to deliver the following:

- Harmonious working relationships with outside experts and world-class contributors to the specialized functional disciplines that the organization needs;
- Identification of organizational members' specialized needs;

- Specialized systems, methodologies, and technologies;
- Methods for communicating, persuading, and educating line managers in new systems, methodologies, and technologies; and
- Methods for indoctrinating the organization in new ideas, systems, methodologies, and technologies; and for training organizational members in their use.

Support Teams

These teams maintain the organization and carry out "off-line" functions such as arranging pensions and running the office cafeteria. Support teams need to deliver the following:

- Specialized support expertise;
- Diagnosis of support needs within the organization; and
- Methods for developing support systems, methodologies, and technologies.

SUGGESTED ACTIVITIES

10. Charting Team Success
11. A Brilliant Future

REFERENCES

Mintzberg, H. (1983). *Structuring in fives.* Englewood Cliffs, NJ: Prentice-Hall.

Roethlisberger, F.J., & Dickson, W.J. (1936). *Management and the worker.* Cambridge, MA: Harvard University Press.

11

Relevant Corporate Role

SURVEY ITEMS

6. Team members are unsure about the team's contribution to the larger organization.

18. Our team's contribution is not clearly understood by other parts of the organization.

30. If the team were disbanded, the organization would not feel the loss.

42. There is confusion between the work of this team and the work of other teams in the organization.

54. The role of our team is not clearly identified within the organization.

66. We do not have an adequate way of establishing our team's objectives and strategies.

78. The organization does not utilize the vision and skills that this team has to offer.

90. The team's objectives have not been related systematically to the objectives of the whole organization.

102. Members would not be able to define exactly what value the team adds to the competitive advantage or excellence of the organization.

Teams exist to serve the interests of the larger organization. A team that lacks a clear understanding of its role cannot fully contribute to the organization's strategic integrity. The resultant dispersal of energy undermines the entire organization. Lack of clarity about its role, and a corresponding lack of a sense of meaning and purpose, weakens a team.

To illustrate this point, consider a team that reports to the vice president for accounting and finance of a medium-sized business. The team members have various responsibilities, such as:

- To the auditors (to provide accurate financial records);
- To the shareholders (to maintain financial propriety);

- To the chief executive officer (to offer expert advice and to provide financial data);
- To managers (to provide useful control data); and
- To the entire organization (to supply creative ideas that will enhance its economic strength).

The team's complete role structure is depicted in Figure 1 below.

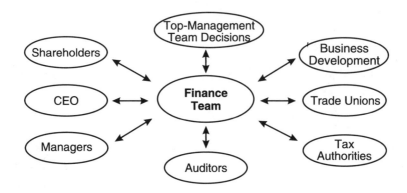

Figure 1. Multiple Roles of an Accounting and Finance Team

The reporting structure for some roles will pull team members in different directions. An accountant's responsibilities to the auditors require whiter-than-white accounting systems. However, the chief executive officer (CEO) may want the accountant to "massage" the figures to gain some short-term advantage. In addition, the need to keep up with the relentless monthly reporting cycle can overwhelm the accountant's desire to supply creative ideas to enhance the economic strength of the company.

When we examine Figure 1 more closely, it becomes apparent that the team members have two types of responsibilities. First, there are well-defined responsibilities to institutions (such as the tax authorities); second, there are more generalized contributions to areas such as "business development" and "top-management team decisions." Each responsibility meets the needs of customers, who make different, sometimes contradictory, requests (see Figure 2).

Teams may find it helpful to draw their own versions of Figure 2. This is best undertaken collaboratively with each of the teams involved, using techniques such as interviews and interteam meetings (see Chapter 17, "Intergroup Relations," for more ideas on developing interteam contracts).

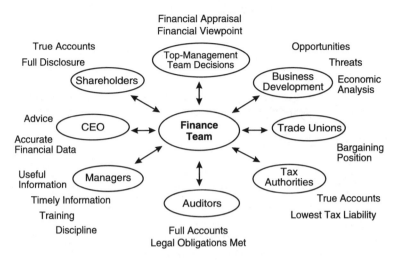

**Figure 2. Multiple Roles of an Accounting and Finance Team
with Customers' Requests**

Because of the often-contradictory demands that are placed on it, each team should establish a procedure for meeting these demands. The following is an outline of a ten-step process.

The team must:

1. Decide who its customers are;

2. Collaborate with customers to identify their needs and wants;

3. Resolve any disputes with customers and clarify their requirements and expectations;

4. Attempt to make win-win deals so that both parties benefit;

5. Establish objectives and success criteria to measure the team's effectiveness in meeting the needs and wants of its customers;

6. Highlight all possible role conflicts and establish conflict-management procedures;

7. Communicate its role definitions to all team members and to all customers;

8. Establish a review procedure to enable roles to be redefined to reflect changes in the team;

9. Develop training programs and appraisal procedures for each team member, based on the needs and wants of each customer; and

10. Define what it needs, as a customer, from the other teams in the organization and negotiate these services team by team.

ESTABLISHING LINKS WITH THE
SENIOR MANAGEMENT TEAM

Organizations are systems that are composed of interlocking and individual teams. The top-management team has two unique roles: to define the roles of the subordinate teams and to integrate the organization. The effectiveness of an organization depends on how well its teams interact with one another in producing the organization's goods and services.

All teams need effective links with the top-management team, which is situated at the strategic apex of the organization. If they are not effective and do not aid communication, these links can lead to disastrous results. For example, one company conducts budget cutting on an annual basis. Usually, in anticipation of the usual budget cuts of 20 to 30 percent, department managers would inflate their estimates to ensure that they would have sufficient resources after the cuts were made. One year, however, the senior management group changed its policy and began to accept budget estimates without making cuts. The result was chaos. The department managers were put in the not-unpleasant position of having to spend their unexpected surplus funds and to justify the expenditures.

Because the managers expected the same policy the following year, they presented budget proposals with no excess at all. However, the senior management group reverted to its previous style to combat the apparent waste and slashed 25 percent from all proposed budgets. More chaos ensued.

This case illustrates how the lack of consistent policies and objectives left managers with little choice but to protect their groups by developing defense mechanisms. If a team's contribution is going to be worthwhile, it must be relevant to the objectives of the larger organization; and those objectives must be understood. Senior teams, therefore, periodically should review their processes of establishing and communicating objectives. Some relevant questions that top managers should ask themselves are:

- How does the team fit into the organization as a whole?
- What contributions does the team make to the organization?
- To what extent does the current system of assessment measure the importance of the team's contributions?
- Are there sufficient mechanisms for clarifying the team's roles?
- What do team members perceive their roles to be? To what extent are their perceptions consistent?

The issues here are more intangible than the more immediate issue of internal team effectiveness. Comparing the two is like comparing a homeowner who is cultivating a yard to a town planner who is responsible for the appearance of the entire community. The appearance of the houses and yards is the responsibility of the individual homeowners, but together, the homeowners' care (or lack thereof) has a profound effect on the neighborhood and on the community at large. It is this type of relationship that must be explored and developed.

It is inevitable that the larger organization will exercise control over its constituent parts. However, the manner and extent of such control often is not clear to the various departments and teams. When excessive direction leads people to feel powerless, their work becomes humdrum and mechanical. Morale is lowered, and "ain't it awful" becomes a constant theme in conversation. Of course, insufficient direction can lead to indecision, to endless duplication of efforts, or to oversights. Teams need to understand fully their contributions to the wider organization, and the organization needs to know and value each team's contribution.

CORE PROCESSES

The core process is the central activity (or activities) that generates key outputs. In a manufacturing organization, the production department has a major role in the core process. In service organizations, core processes generate the services that are purchased by customers. In any organization, all other teams or departments support the core-process group(s). It is important for team members to understand their organization's core processes and their roles in the achievement of key outputs.

When there is overlap in role assignments, problems can arise. Sometimes, actions are duplicated by teams because information has not been shared and without resultant information being shared. Difficulties also occur when there is too much difference in departmental practices (for example, between research-and-development departments ["We want the best technical solution, engineered to the highest standards"] and manufacturing departments ["We need the simplest product, made with the least-expensive materials"]). Steps need to be taken to ensure that teams' value and judgment systems are within the limits that were established for the organization as a whole. Some large organizations, which consist of a head office or group function and various outlying businesses, are faced with the following questions: Whom do we serve? Should we be leading? Controlling? Do we provide a service? Do we have the right to intervene?

VALUE-CHAIN ANALYSIS

Organizational effectiveness results from having a well-balanced system that meets the needs of customers. The value-chain analysis (Porter, 1986) can be of help in understanding how to balance an organizational system. Porter thinks of organizations as systems or chains of teams, each of which (either directly or indirectly) adds value. *Value* is a concept that is used by economists to mean "something that customers are prepared to pay for." Customers determine what value is.

All of a team's activities should add value, either directly or indirectly. Through Porter's analysis, organizations can be viewed as systems of interlinked teams that must operate in harmony. By applying the value-chain theory, a team's activities can be grouped into five direct and four indirect categories. These are:

Direct Activities

Inbound Logistics (IL)	obtaining raw materials
Operations (OP)	transforming raw materials into finished goods or services
Outbound Logistics (OL)	moving finished goods to where they can be sold; supplying services
Sales and Marketing (S & M)	finding out what people want and persuading them to buy a particular product or service
Service (SER)	ensuring that customers receive enduring value from products or services

Indirect Activities

Procurement (PROC)	purchasing the supplies needed to run the firm
Technology (TECH)	the systems, methods, and techniques used to develop products/services, to control, to coordinate, and to set standards
Human Resource Management (HRM)	recruiting, selecting, promoting, rewarding, training, and organizing people
Firm's Infrastructure (FI)	finding funds, determining strategy, and providing overall management

The following questions can be used in beginning a value-chain analysis of an organization.

1. What raw materials does the organization need to operate? What is needed to buy and receive these raw materials?

2. What does the organization produce? What main activities are involved in manufacturing or creating the finished product(s)?

3. How does the organization deliver its finished product(s) to its customers? What steps are involved?

4. How should the organization create a desire for its goods or services (how should it persuade people to buy from it and not from another organization)?

5. What ongoing service does the organization provide? What activities are involved?

6. What equipment, facilities, supplies, etc., does the organization have to buy for each of the activities listed above? What steps are involved?

7. In what research, development, systems, procedures, methods, disciplines, etc., has the organization invested?

8. What activities does the organization undertake to recruit, select, train, develop, motivate, organize, and reward its employees?

9. What activities does the organization undertake to raise capital, to determine its direction, and to set up its basic operating framework?

10. Which of the activities that the organization undertakes are linked with others?

Plot each team's activities on the blank value-chain chart that is depicted in Figure 3 (see next page). It is less important to place each activity accurately than it is to understand how the organization operates as an interlinked series of teams.

Next, place a blank transparency sheet over the completed value-chain chart. Connect interlinked activities with arrows. It is the responsibility of each team to manage its "linkages" with other teams.

These questions can be defined properly only by the organization's top managers, who must be skilled in analyzing, in conducting reviews, and in working with individual teams to ensure that organizational and team goals harmonize as much as possible.

SUGGESTED ACTIVITIES

12. Team Survival
13. Adding Value

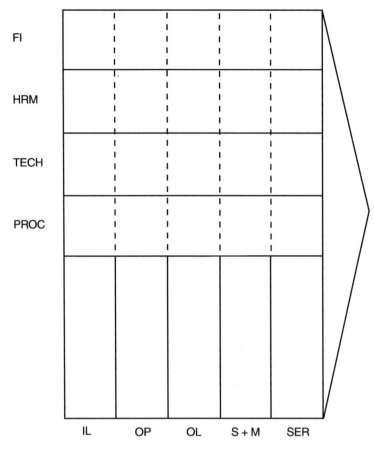

FI

HRM

TECH

PROC

IL   OP   OL   S + M   SER

Figure 3. Value-Chain Chart[6]

REFERENCE

Porter, M. (1986). *Competitive advantage.* New York: The Free Press.

---

[6] Adapted with the permission of The Free Press; a division of Macmillan, Inc., from *Competitive Advantage: Creating and Sustaining Superior Performance* by Michael E. Porter. Copyright © 1985 by Michael E. Porter.

12

Effective Meetings

SURVEY ITEMS

7. We do not achieve much progress in team meetings.
19. During our team meetings, we do not listen to one another.
31. Team meetings lack a methodical approach.
43. Team members do not prepare carefully for meetings.
55. The team does not have an effective means for making decisions in meetings.
67. We seem to get bogged down when a problem is being discussed in team meetings.
79. We have team meetings but do not properly examine their purposes.
91. Decisions that are made at meetings are not recorded properly.
103. Our meetings do not resolve all of the issues that should be addressed.

Meetings are notorious for confused debate, tedious repetition, and ineffective decision making. Much time and many opportunities are wasted during meetings that leave attendees feeling dispirited, confused, or frustrated. However, meetings continue to be "necessary evils" because they often are the only mechanisms by which all factors of a complex issue can be discussed, assessed, and resolved. Important decisions often are made in meetings; therefore, clear communication of meeting outcomes is essential.

Team meetings should allow all members to make contributions and to explore and review issues efficiently. Teams need to learn how to use meetings to develop clarity, commitment, and focused energy for action. Effective meetings ensure that decisions are understood clearly and that individual responsibilities for action are identified.

Effective meetings have the following benefits:

- Important issues are addressed;
- Time is not wasted;

- Team members do not "turn off" and stop contributing;
- High-quality decisions are made; and
- Power is not usurped by cliques.

Every team must develop the following as it progresses toward effectiveness:

- Meeting skills;
- Decision-making techniques; and
- Structured methods of problem solving.

MEETING SKILLS

Some people are much more effective than others in meetings. It is likely that the effective people have mastered the following set of meeting skills:

- Managing the team's process;
- Maintaining discipline;
- Listening actively; and
- Making assertive presentations.

Managing the Team's Process

Management of the team's process requires a set of skills that sometimes is called "chairmanship." We began to explore the topic in Chapter 7, "Choosing the Members of a Team." Each team needs a process manager who controls how the group operates but does not make the decisions. This person should be analytical, observant, and able to elicit the best from people; and also should be controlled, self-confident, calm, and proficient as both a listener and a communicator. The process manager is skilled at:

- Selecting new team members;
- Developing teams;
- Identifying others' strengths and weaknesses;
- Setting or facilitating objectives or terms of reference;
- Supporting the team members;
- Exercising necessary discipline;
- Structuring meetings;
- Clarifying issues;
- Allocating roles to team members; and
- Maintaining momentum toward objectives.

Maintaining Discipline

The ability to maintain discipline (both of oneself and others) is an important skill to have in meetings. Lack of discipline results in:

- Wasted time;
- Domination of the meeting by a few people;
- An excessive amount of time spent on unimportant issues;
- Attendees' irritation, possibly causing them to "turn off";
- An excessive number of issues; and
- Questionable quality of decisions.

In contrast, effective, disciplined teams share the following characteristics:

- All of the team members accept the process manager's authority;
- Members have a shared understanding and acceptance of the structured approach to problem solving and decision making that is described later in this chapter;
- Team members take responsibility for their levels of contribution to the meetings; and
- Teams have a group norm that teamwork always should be productive.

Listening Actively

Listening actively indicates to others that their contributions are respected and valued. It can be particularly helpful in working with people who have diverse opinions. A team whose members practice active listening usually is effective, and its members tend to be eager to participate in meetings.

The process of active listening consists of the following:

- *Checking:* "Can I repeat what you said in order to check my own understanding?"
- *Clarifying:* "It seems to me that this is what you mean:...."
- *Showing Support:* "I hear you. Please continue."
- *Building:* "To your last point I would add the following:...."
- *Structuring:* "Shall we look at the symptoms, try to define the problem, and then discuss possible solutions?"

Teams whose members are not effective, active listeners tend to fall prey to the following:

- Dominance of the team by a few members;

- Cross-talk (several members talk at the same time);
- Ideas are lost because no mechanism for identifying and recording important points exists;
- Contributions are repetitious;
- Wordiness (members speak at length but contribute little);
- Members become bored and disillusioned with meetings; and
- The team is unable to reach consensus in decision making.

Making Assertive Presentations

The ability to make assertive presentations requires an important set of skills. All too often, teamwork deteriorates because some members are unwilling or unable to present their ideas in a cogent or forceful manner. There is a difference between assertion and aggression: the assertive person wants his or her ideas to be heard and considered, whereas the aggressive person intimidates others into doing what he or she wants. The most successful teams consist of strong-minded people who work together without trying to dominate one another.

Assertive presentations are characterized by the following:

- Information and opinions are presented clearly;
- Any members' attempts to dominate are challenged;
- All members express their views clearly and honestly;
- When appropriate, team members clarify their ideas with professional-quality visual aids; and
- Member challenge others' ideas to ensure that concepts and consequences are well thought out.

DECISION-MAKING TECHNIQUES

Some team meetings are ineffective because the members do not understand how decisions will be made. The following anecdote illustrates this point.

One of the authors consulted to the management team of a large, troubled factory. The team leader did not understand why his team was ineffective. After observing the team, the consultant found one clue: some decisions were "command" decisions and were made solely by the leader, but other decisions were "consensus" decisions and were left to the team's discretion. The consultant determined that the team was ineffective because the team members never knew in advance how a decision would be classified. As a result, the members' teamwork floundered.

The consultant suggested that displaying the following chart on the wall of the meeting room would help the team members in the decision-making process. Figure 4 depicts styles of decision making as categories on a continuum.

The factory's management-team leader agreed to make the status of the decision clear to the team members. As soon as the team members understood their roles in the team's decisions, teamwork improved dramatically.

Each of the six decision-making styles that are depicted on the continuum requires the use of a different technique. The decision-making styles toward the top of the figure, which are more directive, require:

- Authority from the team leader;
- Communication and explanation of what should be done;
- Specification of objectives and success criteria;
- Clear definition of individual team members' responsibilities; and
- Definition by the team leader of priorities and time frames.

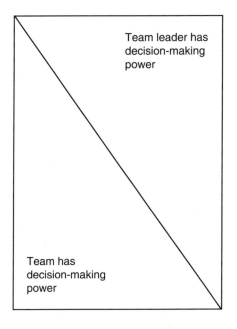

Team leader makes decision and informs subordinates

Team leader asks subordinates for opinions/ information, makes decision, and informs subordinates

Team leader asks subordinates for opinions/ information, makes decision, informs subordinates, and checks for acceptance

Team leader shares the issue with subordinates, asks for suggestions, and accepts or modifies the best proposals

Team leader facilitates subordinates' decision-making process

Team leader delegates decision to subordinates

Figure 4. Styles of Decision Making

The decision-making styles toward the bottom of the figure, which are more participative, require:

- Empowerment of each team member;
- Delegation of the decision to team members;
- A facilitative and catalytic style on the part of the team leader;
- Full participation by all team members; and
- Complete agreement and clarity about how and when decisions will be made.

STRUCTURED METHODS OF PROBLEM SOLVING AND DECISION MAKING

A team is a problem-solving and decision-making unit. Because of the variety of mysteries, assignments, difficulties, opportunities, puzzles, and dilemmas that work teams encounter, team leaders must adopt approaches to problem solving that have structure yet are flexible and adaptable to varying circumstances.

The approach to problem solving and decision making that the authors favor is known by the acronym TOSIDPAR. This approach has eight distinct steps. Each step requires specialized skills and techniques. The process is not rigid; team leaders can adapt the TOSIDPAR approach to their needs. The following paragraphs serve as a brief introduction to the elements of the TOSIDPAR method.

Step 1: Tuning In

The first step in problem solving is to "tune in"—to develop in the members of the team and in all other involved parties a clear, overall appreciation of the issue and its unique challenges. This identification process needs to take place before the team becomes too focused on solving the problem. Members of the problem-solving task force should be chosen on the bases of relevant technical skills, energy, and ability to work well with one another. Roles and responsibilities should be determined, and time constraints and resource limitations should be assessed. At the completion of this step, the team should be able to answer the questions, "What kind of task is this?" and "What challenges does this task present?"

Step 2: Objective Setting

The second step of the TOSIDPAR process is objective setting. In this step, the team members must clarify and state the desired outcome(s) of the problem. This step sometimes is not given the thorough attention that it deserves, as team members usually prefer to take action rather than to clarify objectives. It is the task of the team leader to ensure that objectives are clear, comprehensible, and focused. The aim of this step is to arrive at a shared understanding of the task by identifying both the broad objectives (why the task is being undertaken) and the specific objectives (what goals are to be achieved). The objective-setting step is not complete until all team members understand and support all of the objectives.

Step 3: Setting Criteria for Success

The third step in the process is to define what success on this project will be and to establish how success will be measured. The team leader should emphasize that the assessment step is perhaps the most important part of the TOSIDPAR process. The team must ask (and answer) the following question: "When will we know that we have completed the task successfully?" A clear and specific answer to this question will enable the team to accomplish its task while maximizing its time.

Step 4: Information Collecting

The fourth step in the TOSIDPAR process involves the collection of information—from team members' opinions, facts, feelings, and ideas; and from external data. In many ways, the quality of the team's final decision is a function of its ability to ferret out relevant information and to organize the data. The team must be able to think creatively, to identify relevant data, to collect valid data, to structure data so that it makes sense, and to identify and fill gaps in information. A blend of free-flowing creativity and highly disciplined analysis is required. Step 4 is complete when options for action have been presented.

Step 5: Decision Making

The fifth step in the TOSIDPAR process is the team's assessment of its available options and the making of a decision. In order to do this, the team must formulate and state its options, then state in unambiguous terms what criteria will be used to assess each option. It often is important for the team to distinguish between *essential* and *desirable* criteria. The level of risk involved in each decision also must be assessed. The decision-making step is completed when a decision has been made and communicated to all team members.

Step 6: Planning

In this step, the team formulates a detailed program for implementing its decision. It may be helpful for the team to utilize the military distinction between *strategy* and *tactics*. At the strategic level, broad definitions of What Has To Be Done (WHTBD) are set out; and at the tactical level, specific WHTBDs are addressed. In other words, the team should have both a clear picture of the broad plan and a list of the specific steps and tasks that are included in the plan. Strategies for coping with potential snags (foreseen or unforeseen), coordination, control, communication, specifications, priorities, resource management, and sequencing are vital issues.

Step 7: Acting

Here, plans are put into effect. Tasks are initiated and completed as specified in the team's plans. If the TOSIDPAR approach is followed, the action that the team takes will be relevant to its objectives, and criteria for gauging success will have been developed. Above all, if the previous six steps in this structured approach have been followed carefully, the team members will have sufficient understanding of the reasons behind their actions to be adaptable during the action phase. The word "action" was deliberately chosen over "implementation," which is more passive, to reflect both the roles and the attitudes that are essential during this phase. Of course, if the team has trouble putting its plans into action, it should check itself by repeating the TOSIDPAR process.

Step 8: Reviewing

The eighth and last step in the process gives the team members a structured opportunity to learn from its experience. The purpose of the review is twofold: first, to allow the team to find out if it was successful (whether its specific and measurable objectives were met), and second, to give the team the opportunity to review the entire process so that it can identify its successes and analyze the areas for improvement. Feedback is a crucial element of the review process. Without feedback there is little chance of change and development. The adage "practice makes perfect" is idealistic; a more accurate observation is "practice makes permanent." Unproductive or even detrimental practices can be made as permanent as productive, positive ones. To remain effective, teams must review the cycle of structured problemsolving and decision making continually to winnow out ineffective practices and to build on existing strengths.

Building on the TOSIDPAR approach, we can identify team skills that, grouped together, summarize the essence of effective teamwork. The key skills for effective teamwork are:

- Effective "tuning in";
- Identification of objectives;

- Establishment of criteria with which to measure effectiveness;
- Information-analysis techniques;
- Generation of options for action;
- Comprehensive planning;
- Energetic action;
- Meticulous and honest performance reviews;
- Appropriate controls; and
- Active listening.

TEAM EFFECTIVENESS

The following check list can be used in evaluating the effectiveness of a team.

Task-Effectiveness Check List[7]

1. Does the group use a methodical and structured approach?
2. Are resources (things and people) used effectively?
3. Are ideas and activities coordinated (by a person or a plan)?
4. Do members seek and give information and opinions?
5. Are ideas expanded and tested in the team?
6. Do summarizing and restating of ideas and suggestions occur?
7. Is action initiated, and do members act with energy?

An effective team hones its work methods so that they become disciplined. It gets moving quickly and maintains a rapid pace, but the high level of personal attention and economy of expression ensure that relevant issues are addressed. Individual members develop personal skills that are appreciated and utilized by the entire team. There is an air of competence, and boredom is a rare factor in its meetings.

SUGGESTED ACTIVITIES

14. Astrodome Rescue
15. New Zin Obelisk

---

[7] This check list is based on ideas presented in "Role Functions in a Group," in J.W. Pfeiffer and J.E. Jones (Eds.), *The 1976 Annual Handbook for Group Facilitators,* San Diego, CA: Pfeiffer & Company, 1976, pp. 136-138.

Role Clarity

SURVEY ITEMS

8. The objectives of some team members conflict with those of others.

20. Members of the team do not fully understand one another's roles.

32. There is no regular review of each team member's objectives and priorities.

44. Team members are uncertain about their individual roles in relation to the team.

56. Some team members' roles overlap.

68. I could not, with complete confidence, define my own role within the team.

80. Important work does not get done because no one is responsible for it.

92. Team members could collaborate much more if they would work through their own responsibilities to other team members.

104. Team members fail to resolve role conflicts among themselves.

Adam Smith had some of the most important insights into the nature of teamwork. In his book, *Wealth of Nations* (1977), Smith described how a group of pin makers achieved extraordinary productivity through specialization and the division of labor. If one pin maker had to perform all the steps in the process (heading, polishing, pointing, and so on), he or she could produce only a few pins a day. However, if a team of specialists worked together, they could produce hundreds of pins each day. Their teamwork, which was considered revolutionary, led to the development of the assembly-line system. The system is still an effective one today; watch the kitchen staff in any fast-food restaurant to see it in action.

A visual depiction of this work structure is presented in Figure 5. Each of the boxes in the figure represents one of Adam Smith's pin makers. Raw materials are introduced at the beginning of the process, and the boxes of finished pins are the end products of the process.

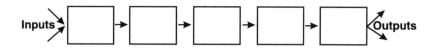

Figure 5. Assembly-Line Work Structure

In the Western world, few teams have such a straightforward structure; automation has taken over many routine, menial tasks. The patterns of interaction among team members have become more complex and can change rapidly. Figure 6 illustrates some of the complicated workings of team interdependence.

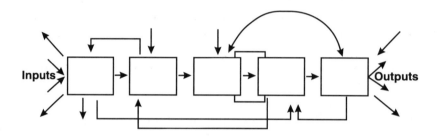

Figure 6. Interdependent-Team Work Structure

When team members function interdependently, the team's effectiveness depends on the extent to which the members do the following:

- Understand their roles in the team;
- Commit to performing their roles well;
- Perform their roles competently;
- Understand the roles of others in the team;
- Develop high-quality relationships with one another; and
- Adapt their roles to suit new requirements and changing needs.

Poor coordination among team members undermines team efficiency and effectiveness. The following example illustrates the importance of coordination.

A married couple operates under a conventional division of labor: he works a standard, five-day work week, and she keeps house, raises the children, and works part-time. If the husband and wife do not communicate about practical matters, things will quickly begin to go wrong. Some bills may be paid twice, and others may not be paid at all. The husband may arrange for the couple to go out with friends on the evening of their child's school play. The wife may decide that both of them will go on a vegetarian diet on the evening that he invites the steak-loving boss for cocktails and dinner. Clearly, this husband and wife need to coordinate their efforts. Put in team-building jargon, there is an urgent need for role clarity.

Lack of role clarity is one of the most troubling blockages that can affect a team—whether it be a married couple or a team of business executives. It is common for managers and subordinates to agree on individual objectives, which usually are formulated using the management-by-objectives (MBO) approach. However, it is much less common to find a team whose members are completely clear about their roles in relation to one another.

Four aspects of role clarity are important to the team builder: an understanding of the concept of role, balance of roles, role negotiation, and role flexibility. Each aspect will be examined in more detail in the sections that follow.

THE CONCEPT OF ROLE

The concept of role was developed by sociologists to explain how organizations function. A role is an explicit definition of the contribution that a person makes to his or her team. Roles are impersonal and do not define or characterize the people who hold them. For example, all people who hold the role of "accountant" perform similar tasks whether they are male or female, introverts or extraverts, Africans or Chinese, twenty-three or sixty years of age. The label "accountant" does not characterize the accountant; the other characteristics do.

Effective teamwork depends on each member's understanding his or her role and the relationships between that role and the other roles held by team members. The nurses and surgeons in an operating room and the crew of a Boeing 747 work as teams because each member has a distinct set of skills and knows what is expected of him or her. In such teams, the team leader's job is to ensure that the team operates according to predetermined patterns. The quality of the team's work is affected by whether the team members adhere to the rules.

When a team's work is less predictable, however, it becomes impossible to work within such rigid rules and roles. An example of this was made by an Army colonel as he reflected on a recent campaign. He said, "The tank crew's job was to perform exactly as it had been trained, but the special forces [that operated behind enemy lines] worked as family units, assessing each situation as it occurred and making decisions as a group." A team that operates in such a diverse environment would be hampered seriously by a fixed and predetermined set of roles. For such teams it is necessary to develop new role definitions for the members as circumstances change.

It is useful to make a distinction between *task* roles and *process* roles. Task roles are those activities that are undertaken to enable the team to achieve its output objectives. Process roles (see Chapter 7, "Choosing the Members of a Team") are those activities that are undertaken to enable the team to function as a harmonious, open, energetic, and effective unit.

If the team adopts a planned program of role definition and defines its primary roles, its process roles, and the ways in which team members can learn through working with others, it will become stronger and more resourceful.

BALANCE OF ROLES

Teamworking skills can be developed through the use of structured experiences such as the activities that are contained in this book. It is fascinating and insightful to observe how people behave when they are given a team challenge. Often, the activity begins with the allocation of tasks; but as the activity proceeds, one or two people work frantically while the others watch and occasionally make comments. Later, when the team members are reviewing the activity, they realize that they failed to allocate roles so that each person was assigned an equal amount of work. There are several reasons that teams fail to obtain maximum input from their members. They are:

- *Historical precedent:* Some team members have always held certain roles and continue to do so.
- *Conformity:* Team members take the roles that are expected of them because of their work experience, job titles, etc.
- *Underdeveloped supervision:* The team leader does not distribute the work load fairly.
- *Poor tuning in:* The team lacks an understanding of the tasks that are being undertaken.
- *Unwilling or incapable team members:* Some people either avoid or cannot cope with the demands of specialized tasks.

Roles also must be balanced with the task in mind. The best team resources and strongest group capabilities need to be directed toward those task elements that are "mission critical." It always pays to ask the question, "What are the activities that we have to do really well?"

Although clear role definition is an important prerequisite to success, it is important not to become exclusionary or overly rigid. Teams thrive on mutual support and interdependence. "It's not my job" is a negative and damaging attitude to have when a colleague needs support. Team members may have individualized roles, but they also should identify the ways in which they can support one another.

In addition, teams usually have task functions (achieving their goals) and process functions (providing effective leadership, structuring work patterns, running meetings, and maintaining morale). A team may pour energy and resources into its front-end activities without considering the required support and administration. This is analogous to an army's moving without supply lines and getting three-quarters of the way to its destination, then discovering that there is no more fuel and food. A team needs to balance the charge toward achievement with adequate administrative support.

ROLE NEGOTIATION

Role contracting and role negotiating inevitably happen in the process of role definition. They are important elements of the team-building process and need to be repeated from time to time during the life of the team.

Contracting is a process in which all the parties in an enterprise explicitly agree what each will give, what each expects to receive and how relationships will be conducted. It often is helpful to write out contracts so that they are clear, comprehensive, and unambiguous. In fact, the act of producing a document to which all involved parties can agree is an essential step in identifying common ground and areas of difference. At the end of an effective contracting process, all the members have "signed up" to work for the team. Wise team leaders know that a contract should balance the needs of the team with the needs of the individual team members. Unless the members feel that they have something to gain by belonging to the team, they will not feel motivated to contribute their energy to the team's goals.

Role negotiation takes contracting one step further through a series of structured discussions designed to foster win-win relationships among team members. Roger Harrison (1972) observed that because team members usually function interdependently, they can learn from looking in detail at the ways in which they can help one another. Each team member, including the team leader, identifies what he or she would like the other team members to do more of, less of, or better. A detailed list is developed, and this serves as the basis for role negotiation.

If team roles are unclear or conflicting, they must be clarified and any role strife must be worked through. One of the most useful techniques for clarifying roles is total quality management (TQM). TQM is a team-centered, team-driven activity (Kinlaw, 1992) in which each role holder is encouraged to think of those who provide information, products, or services as "suppliers" and of those who receive information, products, or services as "customers." Explicit agreements, including criteria for success, are developed with each supplier and customer. Continuous improvement of every aspect of work and business is viewed as the responsibility of all team members. In TQM, customer satisfaction and continuous improvement are shown and proved by *measurement*. Performance appraisal, if it is conducted, is focused on work teams. Awards, if they are given, recognize team achievement rather than individual achievement. The TQM approach formalizes role clarification and is a powerful developmental technique for the team builder.[8]

ROLE FLEXIBILITY

Some jobs allow little, if any, room for role flexibility. An order taker at a fast-food restaurant does not have a flexible role because the organization's mission is to deliver standardized products that meet a very tightly defined set of specifications. In contrast, a police officer on the beat has increased role flexibility, as he or she faces demands that require more autonomy. Around the next corner may be a traffic accident, a lost dog, or a person threatening a busload of terrified passengers. Chief executive officers of major corporations have enormous role flexibility. Some CEOs are reflective, others are action oriented; some are leaders, others are managers.

Therefore, role flexibility should be considered in relation to the particular challenges that face the team. The following guidelines are useful:

- As predictability of tasks increases, team roles usually become increasingly standardized.

- As the members of a team become more interdependent, a comprehensive process of role clarification and role negotiation often is undertaken.

- As the members of a team become more competent, they tend to enjoy a greater degree of initiative and empowerment.

- As the work of the team becomes more complex or creative, ad hoc subgroups often are used.

---

[8] For a more detailed discussion of total quality management, the reader is referred to the following Pfeiffer & Company books: *Continuous Improvement and Measurement for Total Quality: A Team-Based Approach* and *Implementing Total Quality Management: An Overview*. Readers who wish to order these books may write, telephone, or fax the Pfeiffer & Company office from which this book was purchased.

SUGGESTED ACTIVITIES

16. Role Negotiation
17. Airplane

REFERENCES

Harrison, R. (1972). Role negotiation. Privately published paper.

Kinlaw, D.C. (1992). *Continuous improvement and measurement for total quality: A team-based approach.* San Diego, CA: Pfeiffer & Company/Homewood, IL: Business One Irwin.

Smith, A. (1977). *Wealth of nations.* New York: Random House.

14

Positive Critiquing

SURVEY ITEMS

9. When team members are criticized, they feel that they have lost face.
21. Members restrain their critical remarks to avoid rocking the boat.
33. The team is poor at learning from its mistakes.
45. Attempts to review events critically are seen as negative.
57. We would benefit from an impartial assessment of how we work.
69. We lack the skills to review our effectiveness constructively.
81. Performance would improve if constructive criticism were encouraged.
93. Little time is spent on reviewing what the team does, how it works, and how to improve it.
105. We do not learn from our mistakes.

On his return from a conference, a friend told us that he was impressed by a session called "The Learning Organization." He said, "I began to understand what the Japanese mean by *kaizen*. It means that everything can be improved and that we need to stay alert for opportunities to do so. Time has to be set aside to transform experience into learning. The principle that every action provides the seeds for learning is exciting. That is the way to develop the organization."

According to the principles of *kaizen,* teams need to learn from their experiences. The insights that are gained from effective critiques are the raw materials for future improvements. If a review process is not undertaken, the team will be inert. As one disillusioned team member put it, "We simply repeat old errors. The team is, in reality, dead. Nothing changes; we mechanically repeat the same old errors."

In the critique, members of the team analyze the strengths and weaknesses of their individual and collective performances, make open and honest personal assessments, and accept criticism without rancor. The real challenge is for each team member to perceive critique as a valued gift. This can happen only when each team member feels truly accepted by his or her colleagues. Without this sense of commitment to one another, the process of critical analysis can be threatening or even damaging.

The purpose of critique is to enhance individual and team competencies. Critique interferes with the typical action/reaction/action cycle. The leader deliberately introduces the structured-critique process as a "stop" to prevent the repetition of ingrained (and possibly unproductive or even destructive) habits.

Both positive or negative critique must be used with care. Excessive praise can lead group members to unwarranted preening and complacency. Negative comments may be interpreted as sabotage and may provoke a dispute. All too often, critique is given only when things go wrong; the term "post mortem" often is used. Negative-feedback sessions can become "witch hunts" for scapegoats when blame and recrimination occur and when each team member hopes to lie low to avoid being exposed to humiliating criticism. Open critique can be especially threatening to senior team members. As the architects of the existing order, they feel a greater sense of ownership. Hence, their self-esteem can be more at risk.

All too often, teams dash from one thing to the next without taking time to review what they have done. Leaders usually say that they believe in the merits of critique but, in practice, they do not find the time. So the team repeats the same errors time and time again, members' performance remains substandard, and the potential of the team is unexploited.

Critique must assess both success and failure. Unless praise is given with criticism, the critique will fail to energize and nourish the team. On the other hand, some teams appear to operate under an informal conspiracy to criticize little if at all in their reviews. The result of this is the inhibition of the free flow of judgment and commentary that is the raw material for learning. The members of a team may withhold their criticism for several reasons:

- **Politeness:** Team members believe that social etiquette precludes confrontation.
- **Fear of loss of face:** People fear that criticism will erode their self-images.
- **Unwillingness to "rock the boat":** Team members do not want criticism to expose weaknesses or to undermine morale.
- **Inadequate skills:** Team members appreciate the benefits of intensive review but cannot handle it in a constructive manner. They lack the required skills of analysis and personal confrontation.

- *Lack of opportunity:* Insufficient time is allowed for a structured review of the team's performance.

In order for critique to be effective, the team needs to establish clear criteria for success for all of its major activities (both the tasks to be accomplished and the processes by which the team operates). The review process begins with the team members' determining whether they have achieved what they set out to do. They assess whether they have performed as expected, differently than expected, or better than expected. Then comes the important step: to determine the reasons and to decide how to improve in the future. Results are the true test of the efficiency of the team's process. If the team has failed and if the causes are obscure, the team has a issue for analysis and debate.

In reviewing its performance, the team must answer the following twelve questions:

1. Have all of our objectives been achieved?
2. If not, why not?
3. Were all the causes of failure beyond our control?
4. Did we meet our criteria for success?
5. Were our criteria for success relevant and achievable yet challenging?
6. If not, why not?
7. Did we use the minimum necessary resources possible?
8. Did we focus our resources adequately?
9. Have any other individuals or groups tackled similar tasks and done better?
10. If so, why was our performance less effective than those of the other groups?
11. What have we learned from this analysis?
12. What behaviors should we adopt in the future?

Psychologist Barry A. Goodfield supports the value of critique with this statement: "There is a choice. You can advance to growth or retreat to security." People who can use feedback constructively have acquired a valuable asset—they can grow from error or inadequacy.

Initially, critique sessions are best conducted away from the busy and distracting workplace. Later, critiquing skills can be integrated into team meetings and also can be employed informally among team members. The following guidelines may be helpful for facilitating critiquing sessions.

AVOID	TRY TO
Talking too much.	State your points simply and one at a time.
Jumping in and quickly moving on.	Explore ideas and feelings in depth; find concrete examplesof your points.
Glossing over problems.	Explore difficulties and their causes thoroughly, using a "what can we do about this?" approach.
Raising false hopes.	Arrange a contract that you believe is realistic.
Acting "parental" (condescending).	Respond as an "adult" (rationally) rather than as a "parent."
Not taking the process seriously.	Make it evident that you value the process enough to spend time in serious discussion of these issues.
Being inconsistent.	Ask whether you appear inconsistent and clarify all apparent inconsistencies.
Criticizing a person's ambitions or evaluations (the "putdown").	Find out why the person thinks the way that he or she does; contribute information and options rather than judging him or her.
Making commitments too readily.	State the truth, make a commitment only if you are sure that you can honor it, and set a time scale that you know is realistic.
Displaying a negative and disinterested attitude.	Give your support and energy to make a session valuable; try to use the discussion as an important opportunity to improve.
Solving others' problems.	Encourage others to suggest their own solutions and not to depend too much on you.
Using targets as potential weapons.	Set targets for learning rather than for discipline.
Seeing only one way ahead.	Be flexible and look carefully at options, even if you decide to discard them later.

INDIVIDUAL LEARNING

Each team member needs an individual learning review so that he or she can develop a plan for improvement. Without objective feedback, it is difficult for people to rate themselves; they tend either to be excessively lenient on themselves or to ascribe their failings to external rather than internal factors. An effective critique is based on the giving and receiving of feedback. The giver of feedback uses a series of structured techniques, but the most significant aspect of effective feedback is the caring, authenticity, and openness that both parties demonstrate. The purpose of feedback is to develop self-awareness. It enables the receiver to consider whether he or she wishes to change the behavior in question and how he or she could do so. Feedback should be a confronting but not coercive process.

Feedback deals with history—with behavior that has been demonstrated and cannot be changed. The receiver of feedback is therefore vulnerable to feelings of shame, regret, or embarrassment. With this in mind, the giver of feedback should strive to find ways of communicating that strengthen, not demean, the receiver. Every member of a team should become competent in giving and receiving feedback. The aim is to establish a group climate in which people are willing to explore events openly with the intention of learning, not blaming.

The following guidelines are intended to help givers of feedback to be genuinely helpful:

1. ***Be authentic and caring.*** Say what you mean rather than what you think will have the desired effect. Do not try to use the feedback-giving process to manipulate others. Allow enough time for the feedback sessions so that you do not feel rushed. Give them your undivided attention. Try to make feedback sessions open ended.

2. ***Be specific.*** Say what you mean; use specific examples whenever possible. Saying "I didn't think that you made a useful contribution to the meeting" does not help a person to learn. A more specific item of feedback is, "When we came to the issue of scheduling transport, you kept quiet even though you had conducted a comparative study. I felt that your silence deprived us of an important insight into the issue." Focus on *your* feelings about the other person's actions. It is more helpful (and less accusative) to say "When you interrupt me, I feel frustrated" than it is to say "You control all of the group's discussions."

3. ***Be timely.*** The best time to give feedback is as soon as possible after the behavior occurs. Tell people that you will be giving and receiving feedback on a regular basis. Make it part of the team's culture.

4. *Give both positive and negative feedback.* Interestingly, it often is easier to give negative feedback than it is to praise someone. However, people learn from what they do well and need approval to counterbalance critical feedback. Even negative feedback should lead to the statement of a goal for improvement—a positive outcome.

5. *Own the feedback.* The most useful feedback comes directly from the giver, instead of being presented as an objective fact. It is much more useful to say "Your energy at meetings really livens up the group for me" than "you are a lively person."

6. *Be behavioral.* Whenever possible, the focus of feedback should be on *behaviors* that the person can change. Although a person who is told, "I am intimidated by your height," will not be able to change the fact of his or her stature, he or she could act on "Although I am intimidated by your height, it helps me when you sit down for our conversations." Be descriptive rather than evaluative.

7. *Be balanced.* Try not to play the psychological game of "blemish," in which a relatively small aspect of a person's behavior is magnified so that it appears to be a major flaw. Put your comments into a broad context so that the receiver can assess their weight and significance. Suggest that the person compare different aspects of his or her performance with one another, rather than with the performances of other people. Tell people what their performance means to you, to the company, and to the customer. For example: "Each time a customer gets through to a department on the phone but is left waiting for more than a minute, we are in danger of losing a sale."

8. *Adopt good manners.* It may seem old-fashioned, but people report that they feel much happier about receiving feedback when the giver follows the principles of etiquette. In particular, it is essential to treat the other person's feelings as important and not to exploit the sense of personal power that some get when they feel that they have others at a disadvantage. Avoid using strongly authoritarian approaches, which have been shown to be counterproductive. Avoid any overtones of blame or retribution.

9. *Preserve the other person's self-esteem.* No one likes to have his or her ego dented. Involve the receiver of feedback in the detailed identification of his or her weaknesses and strengths.

10. *Accept feedback yourself.* It is important to be open to feedback. Many times, at the end of a feedback session, it is helpful to ask, "How has the session been for you?", "What have the key points from the session been for you?", and "What could I have done differently so that I could have helped you more?"

These guidelines for giving feedback are useful as part of the team's process. Effective feedback is even more essential when the team is confronted with interpersonal difficulties. Utilizing feedback is one of the riskiest strategies available to team-building facilitators, yet it may be the only way to blast through a troubled team's difficulties. Private thoughts are shared in public—a therapeutic but tough process for any team.

Like any powerful tool, feedback can be abused. In particular, feedback either can be given excessively critically or it can be withheld to "punish" another person. The dangers of excessive criticism have been discussed already; one also should consider the dangers of withholding feedback. Everyone, including the team's leader, should be both a giver and a receiver of feedback. By withholding our reactions, we deprive others of information that could be extremely helpful to them. Unexpressed negative thoughts often manifest themselves in behavior that is perceived by others as aloof. Our nonverbal communication or "body language" reveals our true feelings.

One effective feedback technique, which should be used only with groups that agree to the process, is called the "I appreciate/I wish" process and was introduced to the authors by Larry Porter. In this technique, the team members write messages to one another stating what they appreciate about one another and what they would like one another to do differently. The completed messages are signed by their writers. After the messages are distributed, each person should have a message from each team member. Each team member then reads his or her messages aloud and asks for clarification when necessary. Each team member is responsible for any actions or changes that he or she may wish to make in response to the messages.

TEAM-PROCESS EFFECTIVENESS

Critique also must focus on the team's process. Each person who has a role in contributing to the team's analysis of its effectiveness should be asked to respond to the following questions:

- What are the strengths of this team?
- What (if any) skills or competencies does the team lack?
- What aspects of the team's leadership could be improved?
- In what ways could the team's systems be improved?
- What aspects of the team's communication could be improved?
- In what aspects of structured problem solving does the team excel?
- In what aspects of structured problem solving does the team need improvement?

- What processes or activities would help the team to achieve better-quality results?
- What lessons can this team learn for the future?
- Does this team spend more money or use more resources than necessary? If so, please identify the areas of excess.

SUCCESS AND FAILURE

All cultures celebrate success with certain rituals, which serve as sources of nourishment for the human spirit. It is important for a team to take time to celebrate its successes and achievements, whether they be completed projects or interpersonal breakthroughs. Likewise, a team should take the time to examine—and to learn from—its failures. If teamwork goes awry because of human error, the mistakes should be admitted by those who are responsible without recriminations or excuses. The challenge to a team is to turn its failures into opportunities for profound learning without bitterness or accusations. Handled skillfully, the team's sense of disappointment can be transformed into a resolve to do better next time.

SUGGESTED ACTIVITIES

18. Giving Feedback
19. Pluses and Minuses

REFERENCE

Goodfield, B.A. (1971). Quote taken from a meeting with the authors.

15

Personal Development

SURVEY ITEMS

10. No real effort is spent on developing each member of the team.
22. The potential of some team members is not being developed.
34. Team members do not keep up to date.
46. Little time and effort are spent on individual development and training.
58. Team members have been trained only in their technical disciplines.
70. The team does not take steps to develop its members' skills.
82. People who are quiet or uncertain are overridden.
94. Team members are not encouraged to take on new challenges.
106. Individuals are not encouraged to go outside the team to broaden their knowledge and skills.

The effectiveness of a team can be expressed as a simple mathematical formula:

$$A + B + C + D + E = TE$$

"A" represents the contribution of the first team member, "B" represents the contribution of the second team member, and so on. The expression "TE" stands for *team effectiveness*. Overall team effectiveness is a function of two factors: the strength of the team members and the quality of their teamwork, which are expressed as plus signs (+) in the formula. Superior teams are groups of exceptionally able people. As one team leader put it, "In order to make a first-class meal, you must start with first-class ingredients. No matter how talented the chef, a stringy piece of steak cannot be transformed into a great Steak Diane."

Teams have three primary areas of responsibility toward their members: first, to reward the commitment of each member to the team; second, to foster each member's personal growth; and third, to enable each member to gain strength from combining his or her abilities with those of the other members. These areas of responsibility are discussed in the sections that follow.

REWARDING MEMBERS' COMMITMENT TO THE TEAM

We have emphasized the amount of dedication that is required from each member of the team. Almost superhuman commitment sometimes is required. Such loyalty cannot be expected unless participation in the team holds rewards for its members. Team leaders cannot expect members to make extraordinary efforts unless the members feel rewarded and enriched by the team.

An approach called *action-centered leadership* (Adair, 1989), originally developed in the armed services, emphasizes the importance of attending to the needs of each member of the team. The concept of action-centered leadership is illustrated in Figure 7.

The action-centered approach to leadership emphasizes that members must find their membership in the team to be satisfying. The leader needs to understand each person's wants and needs. One team member may seek security and companionship, and another may prize challenge and personal development. These differences need to be understood for the team to be motivated and content. If members' needs are not met—at least in part—motivation will suffer and commitment will deteriorate.

Figure 7. The Action-Centered Leadership Model[9]

---

[9] From J. Adair (1989), *Leadership*. London: Fontana Books.

FOSTERING MEMBERS' PERSONAL GROWTH

Highly developed interpersonal skills and a high degree of emotional maturity are prerequisites for effective teamwork. Ideally, the team should permit—perhaps even encourage—its members to develop personally. Our basic definition of personal development is based on that of Carl Rogers (Kirschenbaum & Henderson, 1990, pp. 306-314), who helped us to identify the following characteristics of a skilled, mature team member:

- *Genuineness:* The person is "real" and says what he or she thinks and feels;
- *Prizing and acceptance:* The team member recognizes that others have importance and value;
- *Empathic understanding:* The team member can "put herself into the other person's shoes";
- *Puzzlement:* The person is truly interested in how his or her team-mates think and feel; and
- *Trust:* The person believes that others will do their best even if they are not being watched.

To help his or her team members to become more mature and more skilled in teamwork, the team leader needs to find ways to:

- Help each member of the team learn to cope with changes, to overcome setbacks, and to continue to grow as a person;
- Help each member of the team to become more self-aware, critical, and questioning;
- Help each member of the team to take on increasingly demanding challenges so that he or she learns through practical experience;
- Provide extensive feedback and personal critique so that each member of the team can come to terms with his or her strengths and weaknesses; and
- Provide constant support, encouragement, and affection to every member of the team.

While conducting research for this book, we asked a group of experienced managers to identify the various approaches to team membership. They agreed that one factor is a predictor of a person's success in a team: how that person uses his or her energy. Some people are predominately passive; others actively express their creativity and energy. The following list emerged from the managers' discussion:

The passive person:

- Seeks not to be disturbed;
- Avoids self-knowledge;
- Is satisfied with sketchy explanations and does not wish to learn about issues in detail;
- Sabotages possible successes;
- Is not in touch with his or her feelings;
- Lacks concern for others;
- Tries to manipulate others;
- Lacks energy and vitality;
- Is generally dissatisfied with others;
- Is unhappy with life;
- Cannot break free from old emotional habits;
- Accepts low standards;
- Gives up to avoid frustration; and
- Finds that he or she cannot concentrate.

The active person:

- Seeks challenge;
- Is insightful;
- Uses his or her time and energy as valuable resources;
- Achieves results;
- Knows and uses his or her feelings creatively;
- Cares for others;
- Is open and basically honest;
- Is not excessively tense physically;
- Usually has a high energy level;
- Generally likes others;
- Enjoys life;
- Is relatively free from childhood "hang-ups";
- Sets high standards;
- Is committed to following through on commitments; and
- Can devote his or her attention to situations.

Few people exhibit either an extremely active or an extremely passive approach to life; most fall somewhere in the middle of the scale. Usually, then, the challenge in development is to move away from the passive end of the scale and toward the active end of the scale. Active people tend to find life an adventure; they enjoy variety and they find something positive in every experience. In contrast, passive people seem always to be in a state of insufficient adjustment to unsatisfactory events.

Personal growth is more likely to happen in teams that have developed a positive learning climate. The following conditions are necessary for a positive learning climate to exist:

- **Commitment:** team members invest energy in creating learning opportunities;
- **Unselfishness:** people go out of their way to understand others and to share their knowledge and skills;
- **Openness:** team members welcome others' variety of experience;
- **Challenge:** all team members are expected to challenge themselves to make their own special contributions to the team;
- **Constructive confrontation:** differences of opinion are aired and resolved;
- **Functional sharing:** team members explain the specifics of their particular positions and tasks, and there is an understanding that all contributions to the team are important; and
- **Interpersonal understanding:** members understand the strengths, weaknesses, and contributions of each person.

STRENGTH IN NUMBERS: COMBINING MEMBERS' ABILITIES

When people join a team, it is important that they are initiated with understanding but firmness. A person should not feel able to "coast" into team membership. The team has to make demands so that membership is considered a privilege. The team becomes a vehicle for personal expression, offering opportunities for each team member to develop his or her technical, leadership, and social skills. A team is like a marriage: the people who are in it need to work to make it succeed and to reap its full benefits.

Team members must take an active responsibility for their own development. In doing so, it is helpful for them to reflect on their contributions by asking, "What did I contribute?", "How well did I make my contribution?", "What else could I have done?", "What was the impact of my contribution on others?", "Did I empower others?", and so on. Perhaps the best way for people to take active responsibility for their development is to develop assertion. When people know what they feel and what they want, take definitive and clear action to present their views, and make sure that they are heard, they are practicing assertive behavior. Assertive people benefit both themselves and their teams.

Teams gain the following from having assertive people as members:

- *Improved decision making:* Incomplete or poorly conceived ideas are screened;
- *More initiatives:* People present more ideas to improve their work and their teams;
- *Better use of resources:* The loudest voice does not always prevail; and
- *True management development:* More active, strong, and promotable talent is recruited and nurtured.

Team members also benefit from assertion because it helps them to do the following:

- *Feel energetic and powerful* because their voices are being heard by others;
- *Get important things done;*
- *Improve the quality of their relationships* because important issues are brought up and worked through; and
- *Express tensions and stressors in constructive ways.*

Although assertive behavior usually is positive and promotes win-win experiences, it sometimes is interpreted negatively. Some people mistake assertive behavior for aggressive behavior, in which a person attempts to get his or her own way by intimidating, coercing, or otherwise pressuring the other person in an emotional or physical way. (In contrast, assertion is based on respect for others' rights and points of view.) Assertive people are forthright with their opinions, which may leave them open to ridicule. Some people may perceive assertive people as nuisances (or, at worst, as obstinate troublemakers) and may take action against them. Of course, assertion is not appropriate in every situation, and people who wish to practice assertive behavior must use good judgment and tact in doing so.

Although they may realize that it is logical and empowering to be assertive, some people find it very difficult. The items below list some common reasons that people find themselves unable or unwilling to be assertive. People may find that they fear or resist assertion for different reasons with different people.

1. *Upbringing:* many people were brought up with the credo that it is impolite to criticize others, particularly those who are older or who are "more important" or "more knowledgeable."

2. *A sense that "what I say isn't important":* a person who wishes to be assertive must believe that he or she has the right to be heard and taken seriously. However, some people believe that they are unintelligent or that they lack creativity and that their opinions are worth less than those of others.

3. *Lack of clarity of purpose:* if people do not know what they want from themselves and from others, they probably will be unable to express themselves clearly and convincingly.

4. *Fear:* assertive statements may annoy or be criticized by others. People who fear disapproval or punishment usually will not be assertive.

5. *The "doormat" syndrome:* if a person seeks to please others even if doing so means allowing others' reactions or circumstances to weaken or squelch his or her efforts or beliefs, that person is likely to be incapable of assertion.

Some people seem to get their points across in a group setting much more effectively than others. Some tips for assertive presentation are listed here.

1. *Avoid overt display of emotion.* Being angry or hurt can take energy away from the message and the goal. A rational, straightforward presentation is best.

2. *Deal with one issue at a time.* You will be less effective if you try to deal with many issues at once, and the importance of each issue will be dimmed. Instead, focus on one point and be persistent until the matter is resolved. Back down only when you make a rational decision that progress is impossible.

3. *Be clear and direct.* Lack of clarity blunts a message. A confusing issue that is presented in a roundabout manner is difficult to resolve.

4. *Convey your conviction about the issue.* Although excessive displays of emotion can be counterproductive, it is important to let others know how strongly you feel about the matter. Be honest, though; avoid exaggeration or false humility.

5. *Avoid being sidetracked.* Other people may try to divert attention from your issue in an attempt to thwart you or to defend themselves from scrutiny. The best way to deal with such people is to let them say their piece and then to return to your point.

6. *Be assertive, not aggressive.* Other people are entitled to their opinions, even if they differ from yours. Accept the truths in opposing arguments, but stand by your basic viewpoints.

7. *Admit error openly.* If you are wrong, say so openly and directly. If you make a mistake, be strong and try to learn from the error.

8. *Go for the workable compromise.* Win-win relationships are especially fruitful. To create them, identify other people's needs and try to meet both them and your own during negotiations. When you do so, both you and the other person win.

Assertive people are strong resources who feel good about themselves and their jobs. Like all strengths, however, assertion can be abused, and strong-minded members can place special strains on the leader and on their teams. Some members of the team may feel threatened by others' assertive behavior, so the mature team will take care to develop the competencies and strengths of *all* of its members. Even so, the team will benefit, as conformity through abdication is unlikely, and agreement on decisions is more likely to be genuine.

Personal development is difficult to define because the process is a personal one and the outcomes are hard to measure. The psychologically developed person is open and curious. Over time, the person becomes less discriminatory and less enchanted with novelties and fads. Concurrently, the person's capacity for new insights increases. After exploring what he or she values and believes in, the mature, developed person accepts and allows the expression of beliefs that are different from his or her own.

SUGGESTED ACTIVITIES

20. People-Skills Inventory
21. Good Coaching Practice

REFERENCES

Adair, J. (1989). *Leadership.* London: Fontana Books.

Kirschenbaum, H., & Henderson, V.L. (Eds.). (1990). *The Carl Rogers reader.* London: Constable.

Team Creativity

SURVEY ITEMS

11. Not many new ideas are generated by the team.
23. Team members are wary about suggesting new ideas.
35. This team does not have a reputation for being innovative.
47. This team seldom is innovative.
59. Good ideas seem to get lost.
71. New ideas from outside the team are not accepted.
83. It would be fair to say that the team has little vision.
95. Only a few members suggest new ideas.
107. Creative ideas often are not followed up with definite action.

It is said that Albert Einstein developed the concept of the curvature of space while daydreaming about riding on a sunbeam. During World War II, a British scientist invented a bomb that would skip like a stone along the surface of the water before exploding against the restraining walls of German dams. Such concepts and inventions are the work of brilliant, creative people. However, progress could not be made if only those few people were asked to do the work. Consider the tasks of mapping the shape of the human DNA chain and of finding cures for our many genetic illnesses. Thousands of scientists, working in hundreds of teams in laboratories around the world, are involved in these tasks.

Clearly, not all breakthroughs are the products of single minds. Teams can be extremely creative, particularly when they function so that "the whole is greater than the sum of the parts" (together, the members can be more creative than if each member worked alone). We believe that, if they are effective, all teams can generate creative ideas and put them into practice.

The process of creation is hard to describe in rational and objective terms. People often are unable to explain how ideas came to them. One is likely to hear that "It came to me in a dream" or that "Everything suddenly clicked." Edward Matchett (1976), a British researcher who has studied the creative process intensively, reports that people can learn to develop their creative potential by "tuning in" to latent aspects of themselves. His research indicates that creativity is aided when people are emotionally, physically, and intellectually open to new ideas and experiences.

Despite the "it just happened" phenomenon, creativity does not have to be unplanned or haphazard. Teams can enhance their creativity with the use of relatively straightforward techniques. We see the creative process as beginning with the identification first of a need and then of the "missing links" between the status quo and the realization of the idea. Next, a new idea is needed. The new idea can be anything from a logical extension of an existing process to a radical departure. Seldom is a new idea clear or fully developed at its inception; it has to be fleshed out, enlarged, extended, and simplified.

Some ideas come from unexpected sources. Scientists in Virginia are studying the flounder, a flat fish that can survive in subfreezing temperatures and whose system contains a natural antifreeze. Their studies may result in such products as materials for preventing road icing and frost-resistant crops. Other researchers, who discovered that the sperm of the male herring contains a chemical that resists the AIDS virus, used their findings in developing the first effective anti-AIDS drug, AZT.

For a team to be creative, its members must question their habits and assumptions. Innovative thinking should be encouraged and managed, and all ideas should be explored and evaluated. Risk taking (with no recriminations) must be encouraged. Methods of researching new ideas need to be established.

A team climate that encourages creativity and risk taking also improves the work environment. The team will be less likely to become rigid and fearful of change. An effective, innovative team attracts creative people who will contribute new ideas. This keeps the team members challenged and confident.

If the following items are true for your team, it is likely to be low in creativity.

- Assumptions, values, and habits are not challenged;
- Change is not encouraged or welcomed;
- Adaptation to new challenges or circumstances is slow;
- Innovative members are demotivated;
- Team members' energy is low; and

- The team is perceived as pedestrian by other teams.

Risk cannot be eliminated from creativity, and the most highly trained and experienced people will make errors. Accordingly, a climate that encourages creativity must include the norm that a level of failure is normal and acceptable.

BLOCKS TO CREATIVITY

In exploring the process of developing creativity, it is useful to begin with the ways in which people are prevented from being more creative. Common blocks to creativity and innovation can be summarized under the following five headings.

Block 1: Rigid Mind Set

Most people interpret their experiences according to their personal views of the world. Of course, it is easier to see this rigidity in others than in oneself. Unfortunately, the process of defining and judging ideas, events, and other people tends to rule out the questioning of well-established ways of thinking. In fact, rigid attitudes become more so with the passage of time because they are self-fulfilling. People "filter" their interpretations of experiences so that the experiences justify their attitudes and beliefs.

Block 2: Poor Presentation Skills

People who are trying to express new ideas often are unclear, repetitious, or inconsistent. The excitement and anxiety about the new idea can interfere with presentation skills. Speakers also may be so worried about their presentations that they overlook the needs of the people who are listening to them.

The process of *active communication* can help presenters to get their messages across clearly and with sensitivity to their listeners. First, the presenter must be attuned to the needs of the person to whom the presentation will be made. The receiver's level of understanding, beliefs, and relationship with the presenter all will affect how he or she receives the message. The time and place of the presentation also need to be considered. Some issues can be worked through rapidly, but more time is needed to deal effectively with issues that are complex or personal. The place of the meeting should be appropriate to the issue's levels of importance and confidentiality.

The presenter should ensure that the other person is receptive by asking, "Do you have time to talk with me about this topic?" By doing so, an agreement is made, and the conversation is identified as important.

In beginning the presentation, it is helpful for the presenter briefly to identify the purpose of the session and to clarify the needs, wants, and expectations of the listener(s). The speaker should watch for nonverbal signals that his or her message is being received. A more direct check can be done by inviting comments or questions. Sometimes it is helpful to the audience if the presenter can visually display the information or idea on a flip chart or an overhead projector.

Several mistakes are common to neophyte presenters; all are likely to frustrate and "turn off" an audience. They are:

- Inappropriate timing in conversations;
- Lack of specification of the purpose of the conversation;
- Repetitious and wordy speech;
- Failure to check with the listeners for understanding;
- Lack of focus and a rambling style of presentation; and
- Critical and argumentative reactions.

Block 3: Lack of Open Expression

Much creativity stems from the discontent of people who perceive that present systems, methods, or products are inadequate. Their critical evaluations spark the energy to initiate change.

People often speak as if openness is achieved easily, but this is untrue. Although some kinds of open expression, such as giving praise, are easy to do, it is much more difficult to bring up matters that appear to be unresolvable, improper to discuss, or closed. Many people find it difficult to be open about negative things, especially to the people who are responsible for them. If they choose to say anything at all, their criticisms probably will be muted and generalized and thereby will have less impact.

Decisions are made every day by people who limit the extent to which they are open and who restrain themselves from expressing their opinions. Such people need to develop the capacity to be more open more often. If this is not done, they will lose some of their confidence and self-responsibility, and their creativity will be stunted.

Someone who is attempting to be more open about problems often will say, "I don't know where to begin." What this person needs to do is to begin anywhere. Out of his or her expressions of difficulty and emotion can come new energy to solve problems and manage progress.

Block 4: Inadequate Techniques for Generating Creativity

Applied creativity is partly discipline and technique. Because most creative techniques are relatively straightforward, they are, unfortunately, scorned by many. However, the following three methods help considerably:

Brainstorming

Brainstorming is a well-known tactic for generating ideas in a group. In brainstorming, the process of generating ideas is separated from the process of evaluating them. Instead of evaluating (or criticizing) ideas as they are suggested, the group suggests as many ideas as it can during a specified period of time, and one member records them for a later evaluation session. Criticism is not allowed during the idea-generation phase. Using this technique, a group can generate a large quantity of ideas rapidly. (See Activity 22, "Team Brainstorming," for a more complete description of this technique.)

Mind Maps

Mind maps, which are most easily read by those who prepare them, offer a creative and rapid technique for generating ideas (Buzan, 1974). This technique can speed a team's progress in acquiring, collating, and structuring information by doing the following:

- Preventing ideas from getting lost;
- Stimulating individual and group creativity;
- Decreasing the amount of unnecessary repetition;
- Clarifying links between ideas; and
- Highlighting areas in which the team has insufficient information.

Figure 8, which shows how one person used the mind-map approach to capture the key concepts in team building, demonstrates the primary uses of the mind map. The information in the mind map is arranged to facilitate the brain's comprehension of patterns and key ideas. Key words are used to catch the essence of ideas, and relationships and key points are easy to see. Color may be added to the map for additional emphasis and clarity.

The Why/How Chart

One of the most interesting problem-solving techniques is known as the why/how chart. The why/how chart combines the brainstorming and mind-map techniques with a third concept, *tiers of objectives*. It is insufficient to consider only general objectives (e.g., "to improve the environment"), but to concentrate only on specific activities (e.g., "ride my bicycle to work") can mean that one loses sight of their purpose. An example of the relationships between direction statements is depicted in Figure 9 (see page 151). The

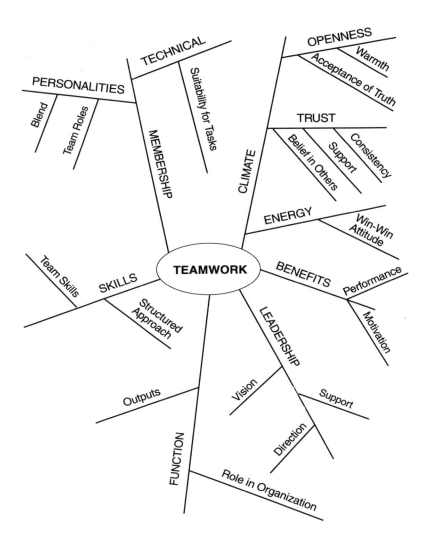

Figure 8. A Team-Building Mind Map

why/how chart is relevant to the creative process because, to be innovative, all tiers of objectives must be considered.

Block 5: Organizational Support

A team cannot be creative and innovative without the support and encouragement of organizational management. Some organizations are exciting,

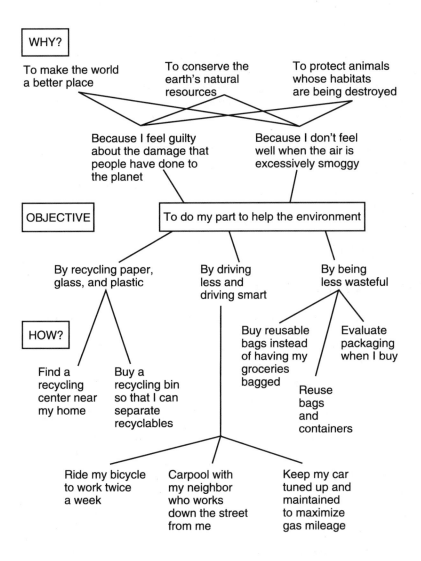

Figure 9. Sample Why/How Chart

stimulating workplaces; others stifle the creative impulses of their employees. The repetition of meaningless tasks increases workers' frustration and stifles their vitality, enthusiasm, and creativity. This type of climate is dangerous to an organization's health because it deprives it of creative potential and increases employees' resistance to change.

Especially in organizations in which innovation is considered a rare talent and is required from only a select few employees, change is frowned on, and countless valuable ideas go unnoticed or unsaid.

A key task of management is to release the latent energy in the work force. To be effective, managerial support of innovation should include the following norms:

- Each person's ideas and work have value;
- Ideas, not people, are criticized;
- People listen to one another's problems and frustrations with their work;
- Adequate resources for the testing of ideas are provided; and
- People are not punished if things go wrong.

THE CREATIVE TEAM

Creative teams in supportive organizations share the following qualities:

- **Radicalism:** members can put aside conventional wisdom to challenge orthodox ways of thinking and acting;
- **Support for diversity:** creative people are encouraged to contribute to the team;
- **Risk taking:** the team experiments and learns from its experiences;
- **Creative culture:** "the way we do things around here" is to question the status quo and to seek ways to make improvements;
- **Open-mindedness:** tolerance of and openness to others' ideas are encouraged;
- **Rewards for creativity:** the organization's reward system supports creativity and innovation; and
- **Creative techniques:** the team's ways of working increase its creative potential.

When an organization supports creativity, the creative urge spreads rapidly. Even though not all jobs contain equal opportunities for creativity, all can benefit from creative approaches and innovative thinking.

SUGGESTED ACTIVITIES

22. Team Brainstorming
23. Creative Attitudes

REFERENCES

Buzan, T. (1974). *Use your head.* London: BBC Publications.

Matchett, E., & Trevelyan, G. (1976). *Twelve seats at the round table.* Jersey, U.K.: Neville Speerman.

Interteam Relationships

SURVEY ITEMS

12. Conflicts between our team and other groups are quite common.
24. Our team does not have constructive relationships with some of the other teams within the organization.
36. The team does not respond sufficiently to the needs of other teams in the organization.
48. We do not actively seek to develop our working relationships with other teams.
60. Significant mistakes could be avoided if we had better communication with other teams.
72. In this organization, teams and departments tend to compete rather than to collaborate.
84. Other teams/departments have a low opinion of us.
96. We do not get to know the people who work in other teams in the organization.
108. If we worked better with other teams in the organization, it would help us all to be more effective.

The members of a team often are required to interact with people and groups other than themselves. Such relationships are crucial to organizational success but rarely are as smooth and as productive as they could be. Some interteam relationships are unconstructive or even hostile.

We have used the Team-Review Survey with thousands of managers over the years. Of the twelve blocks to team effectiveness that can be identified through use of the survey, unconstructive interteam relations has been selected as the most significant team issue (i.e., the most problematic) most frequently. For many teams, interteam relations is the primary area in which they must improve.

Before one can attack the problem of poor interteam relations, one first must identify the traits that characterize teams that work well together. They are as follows:

1. The teams share objectives and priorities.
2. The team members feel a strong need to pull together.
3. The teams share a vision of the future.
4. There are no conflicting objectives among teams.
5. The teams are evaluated in ways that bond them together.
6. The teams' members know one another personally.
7. The teams' managers demonstrate helpful attitudes to one another.
8. A full discussion takes place whenever one team is planning an action that may affect the other team(s).
9. There is open communication among teams.
10. The members of one team do not disparage the members of the other team(s).
11. The teams often hold joint meetings in which to discuss and resolve any difficulties.
12. Formal systems to promote efficient, effective communication exist.

Some teams have poor relationships with other teams simply because no one has looked systematically for areas in which improvements can be made. It is common for teams to participate in team-building events, but structured interteam sessions are rare. Many team leaders lack processes or systems for improving interteam relations. In this chapter, we will examine some of the key reasons that teams fail to work well with others and what can be done to improve interteam relationships.

COMPETITION

Teams frequently engage in competition that may be disguised but rarely is irrelevant. Although much energy and concern are invested in such competition, it often is difficult to detect because it manifests itself as a subtle undercurrent that is expressed only obliquely and indirectly.

Furthermore, people often talk about their work in sports- or war-related terms. They speak of playing to win, of scoring points, and of identifying the name of the game. They may even talk about screwing the members of the opposition, of beating them into the ground, and of kicking them when they are down. Such expressions reveal how people think about their work and what mental images they use.

Western society places a great emphasis on winning, on defeating others, and on being the champion. When teams in an organization think of one another in such competitive terms, they set up win-lose expectations. (Both teams cannot win; if one team wins, the other team must lose.) When one team strives to "win" at the expense of another, the results are costly. Communication may be severely limited, close relationships may be severed, and the "loser's" contributions may be downgraded by the "winner." There also are costs to the organization as a whole. In addition, labels—such as "winner" and "loser"—often are self-fulfilling. Industrial psychologists who have observed the process of labeling and stereotyping report that people tend to accept their labels and to act as if they were true.

It is especially difficult to promote openness between teams at different hierarchical levels. Teams almost always are arranged in a hierarchy, and those that are higher in the structure often find themselves unable to obtain honest, clear, and open communication from those that are beneath them. When senior teams take the roles of arbiters, inquisitors, and angels of retribution, subordinate teams quickly learn to cover their tracks and to defend their territories.

DEVELOPING INTERTEAM RELATIONS

Teams may regard one another as neutral but still fail to communicate well. If this is the case, the fault lies with the methods of communication used, not with the members' attitudes. The teams should make a conscious effort to develop a relationship, to identify common objectives, and to improve the minutiae of routine contact. It is helpful for the teams to bring any difficulties to the surface so that they can be discussed and resolved.

The process of improving interteam relationships requires conscious planning and the creation of opportunities that may not present themselves readily in day-to-day organizational life. The process of improving interteam relationships includes the steps that are described in the sections that follow.

Step 1: Identify the Teams' Common Objectives

In an organization, teams often are unclear about other teams' objectives and outputs. (Although an objective such as "make more profit" could be construed as a common organizational goal, it is far too superficial to be useful.) Objectives should be explicit and detailed. Teams need to know in what ways they depend on others within the organization. They need to share and compare objectives to identify overlaps and differences; if they do not, their relationship may degenerate into formal sniping via memoranda.

Step 2: Gain a Personal Understanding of One Another

If members of different teams get to know one another on a more personal basis, they will be much more eager to work together and to think of one another when they are making decisions. The need for personal contact becomes greater when the possibility of conflict exists.

Members of teams that interact need to feel that they understand one another's motivations and driving forces. One department manager said the following about his team's relations with another department: "After our meeting, I felt that we understood you much more as people. We understood your motives and felt sympathy for you. How we could help you and how you could help us became clear. We needed the information about who you are, how you work, and whether you actually do what you say you will do. As soon as these questions were answered, the rest fell into place."

Step 3: Develop Systems of Interacting

Most large organizations do not have sufficient processes for working through interteam issues and problems. In this respect, organizations are frequently immature and need systems that foster high-quality communication and interaction among teams and departments. Before such methods can be created, of course, it must be decided that they are needed and that appropriate time and resources will be allocated to their development. A preliminary assessment of the needs of the groups involved is a necessary first step.

Step 4: Manage Team Boundaries

Boundaries between teams must be managed. The management of team boundaries may require anything from formal mechanisms to opportunities for informal communication. In one case, the manager of a food factory was driven almost to despair by the acrimonious and negative relations between the factory engineers and the purchasing department. The manager's solution was to move both groups into one large office. As they interacted informally, the boundaries "melted."

In other situations, more formal mechanisms are required to manage team boundaries. It often happens that one or two people act as "diplomats" to represent their teams in interactions with others. The selection and briefing of these representatives is of great importance because others base their impressions of the teams on their impressions of the representatives.

Step 5: Build a Climate of Trust

Trust is based on honesty—the disclosure of one's intentions and methods. Trust is built between people who work through difficult situations together and assess one another's characters while doing so. Teams that want to develop open and trusting relationships with other teams will have to expose both their strengths and their weaknesses. They need to demonstrate that they are prepared to face difficult issues and to work them through. They also must try to be consistent and to follow through on their promises.

THE TEAM AS PART OF A SYSTEM

Organizations are systems. Each element of a system is like a link in a chain, and a chain is only as strong as its weakest link. In a productive organization, teams work together to capitalize on their collective strength. Organizational success requires a well-balanced system of interdependent teams that meets the needs of customers.

The following ideas form the basis for a system-based theory of interteam relations:

1. Organizations can be likened to living organisms.
2. The whole organism or system consists of a series of parts. Each part plays an important role in the overall functioning of the system.
3. If a part of the system is internally defective, it will damage the organism.
4. If the parts are not sympathetic to one another and do not work together in a complementary fashion, the organism will suffer. If the discord is serious, the organism may break up and cease to exist.
5. A key factor in maintaining a healthy organism is for the boundaries that exist among its parts to remain open, thus allowing for the exchange of "nutrients" and information. If the boundaries are closed, the organism will wither and possibly may die.

A Case Study

Interteam relationships can be improved in most organizations—with substantial benefits. However, many managers lack the necessary skills to do so, because they are unable to develop constructive relationships with people who operate outside their boundaries. The problem is illustrated in the following case history.

> A large department (Department A) of a food-manufacturing business converted raw materials into a intermediate product, which then was passed on to another process unit (Department B) for conversion into the final packaged goods. The company hired a new factory manager who was intent on reducing costs. After reviewing the objectives of Department A, the new manager set some stiff cost-reduction targets for the department. Department A's manager gathered his supervisors around him and explained the situation. Because the department's biggest cost was raw

materials, he suggested an effort to conserve raw materials and to cut tolerances to the bone. The supervisors, who were old hands and who respected their boss, set to work willingly. After three months, Department A had saved the organization nearly $100,000. The department's team members congratulated themselves on their success and started making plans for spending their anticipated merit raises.

It was also at this three-month stage that the factory manager began hearing complaints from Department B that their reject rate was rocketing because of defective and underweight raw materials. At the end of six months, Department A had met its cost-reduction targets and had saved over $300,000. But during the plant's year-end review, it was discovered that Department B's losses because of rejection and rework had exceeded $400,000. The outcome: the plant had lost $100,000. Department A had succeeded in meeting its team goals, but the result was that Department B and the plant both lost.

Management teams need clear signals from others to let them know whether they are on the right track. This caveat applies most strongly to teams that provide services to other parts of their organization.

Some teams can become so involved in studying their internal functioning that the state of their boundaries becomes a matter of low concern. This can be risky, particularly if teams deliberately close themselves off from others in the organization and escalate competition to "beat" teams that they perceive as rivals.

Teams that work well together strengthen the entire organization. Each team has both internal suppliers and internal customers. As teams learn to collaborate, they overcome insularity and narrow thinking. Interteam development actually strengthens the individual teams.

SUGGESTED ACTIVITIES

24. Castles in the Air
25. Interteam Mapping

Part 4:

Addressing Blockages: Activities

Introduction to the Activities

This part of the book moves from exploration to action. At this point, the team is aware of both its strengths and the blockages that it has chosen to address. Facilitators have developed many projects and activities (called *structured experiences*) that are designed to help teams to "unblock" themselves. Part 4 of this book contains twenty-five activities that have proven useful in team-building programs. The first activity is an introductory activity; each successive activity is directly related to one of the twelve key team blockages that was explored in the earlier parts of this book.

DESIGNING A TEAM-BUILDING PROGRAM

The team leader should begin by examining each activity thoroughly and determining which ones meet the team's needs at this time. In our experience, teams find at least half of these activities valuable, but different teams prefer different activities.

An activity approach to team building enables a team to assemble a program to suit its particular needs. However, there is a risk that trying one activity after another can fragment a team's efforts. To avoid this, we suggest that the team select and conduct a sequence of three or more activities. Participation in the process increases the team members' commitment to the program. The value of the activities is further increased if the team takes an hour for review when the initial program of activities has been completed.

Off-Site Team Building

Team building often is best conducted away from day-to-day work pressures. An off-site team-building session offers the team members the opportunity to do a methodical review and creative planning. The following guidelines may be useful in planning such a session.

1. Plan the schedule with the following formula in mind: Each extra day that is allotted to team building generally doubles the value of the session to the participants (up to three days).

2. Meet with the team before the session to establish objectives and to determine criteria for measuring success.

3. Choose a sequence of activities that meet the established objectives, beginning with the more straightforward activities. Use the activities' time guidelines to construct a schedule for the session.

4. Engage the services of a skilled team-building consultant if the team is moving into uncharted waters or if significant interpersonal issues will be addressed.

5. As much as possible, arrange the team's working sessions so that members will not be interrupted.

6. Relax and enjoy the session. Team building should be fun!

USING THE ACTIVITIES

The following guidelines will help the team leader to use the activities in this book successfully.

1. Identify the activities that correspond to the blockages that the team members chose to address after completing the Team-Review Survey. (The Index to Activities indicates which activities were designed to address the blockages.) Pay particular attention to the activity ratings in the index.

2. As a team, review the activities (and any others that the team wishes to include, such as those published in Pfeiffer & Company's *Annual* series or in its *Handbooks of Structured Experiences for Human Relations Training)* before making final selections. List the selections in order of priority.

3. As each activity comes with detailed, step-by-step instructions, the person who will lead the activities (the team leader or an outside facilitator) should familiarize himself or herself with the processes. Sufficient preparation is necessary for the success of the team-building session.

4. The team will need a private room that is quiet, free from distractions, and adequately ventilated. Seating should be comfortable, and tables should be provided if they are specified in the "Materials" section of the activity. The room should have enough wall space so that the facilitator can post newsprint sheets.

5. Adhere to the process suggested in the selected activity whenever possible.

6. Allow sufficient time for team members to discuss the experience after completing an activity so that feelings can be expressed and any uncertainties or questions can be resolved.
7. Try to ensure that the team members will not be interrupted during the team-building session.

Index to Activities

The following index lists the title of each activity, the team blockage to which the activity relates, and a brief description of the goals of the activity. Each activity also is assigned one or more ratings. The ratings are as follow:

Symbol	Explanation of Rating
F	Activities that require the giving or receiving of feedback. Before a team begins any of these activities, we suggest that it complete Activity 18, "Giving Feedback."
1	Straightforward activities that can be incorporated into normal team operations with little or no preparation or outside assistance.
2	Activities that may raise sensitive or interpersonal issues. Before beginning these activities, the team members should review them carefully and voluntarily agree to participate.
3	Advanced activities that are likely to bring out sensitive issues that may affect the entire team or certain members. Before beginning these activities, the team members should review them carefully and voluntarily agree to participate. It also is useful for the team members to consider the following before undertaking a category-3 activity:

- Are we prepared to face issues that may be sensitive and that may cause some members discomfort?

- Would the risks of undertaking such an activity be reduced if a skilled outside facilitator were available to help us work through any sensitive issues that may arise?

ACTIVITY	RATING	USE WITH TEAM BLOCKAGE	GOALS
1. Setting Team-Building Objectives	1	Introductory	To clarify a team's development needs. To set objectives for team development and to establish criteria for measuring success. To provide a framework for beginning a team-building program.
2. Leadership-Functions Analysis	F, 2	Leadership	To help the team to understand how leadership functions currently are carried out in the team. To determine the best ways of carrying out leadership functions in the team.
3. The Leadership-Style Profile	F, 1	Leadership	To clarify the team leader's leadership style. To give team members the opportunity to give feedback to their team leader. To help the team leader plan how to build on his or her leadership strengths and to address any desired leadership improvements.
4. Team-Roles Analysis Questionnaire	F, 1	Membership	To give the team members an opportunity to discuss the different ways that people contribute to teams. To foster the team members' respect for one another's differences. To help the team members to find ways to enhance their contributions to the team.
5. Use Us—We're the Best	1	Membership	To critically review the skills, capabilities, and potential of a team. To evaluate the market-ability of a team.
6. Team-Development Stages	2	Commitment	To enable a team to evaluate its current stage of development. To offer the team members the opportunity to set priorities for the team's development. To help team members to evaluate their levels of commitment to the development of the team.

ACTIVITY	RATING	USE WITH TEAM BLOCKAGE	GOALS
7. Designing a Team-Building Workshop	1	Commitment	To allow the team members to participate in defining the objectives and content of a planned team-building workshop. To plan the team-building workshop so that it will utilize the members' time most efficiently.
8. The Team-Climate Questionnaire	F, 2	Climate	To give the team the opportunity to examine its working climate and to prepare an action plan for improving it.
9. Fong Construction: A Study in Teamwork	1	Climate	To give the team members the opportunity to explore the fundamental causes of ineffective teamwork. To develop the team members' capacity to analyze their team's climate. To give the team members the opportunity to explore the techniques of effective chairmanship. To give the team members the opportunity to critique their team's skills, capabilities, and potential.
10. Charting Team Success	2	Achievement	To examine the team's recent achievements. To give the team members the opportunity to consider the forces (internal or external) that influence the success or failure of a team.
11. A Brilliant Future	1	Achievement	To explore any barriers toward team achievement that the members may have. To motivate team members toward higher achievement.
12. Team Survival	1	Corporate Role	To give the team a method of justifying its existence to the broader organization.

ACTIVITY	RATING	USE WITH TEAM BLOCKAGE	GOALS
13. Adding Value	1	Corporate Role	To give the team members an opportunity to explore the concepts of value, of the value chain, and of adding value. To present a systematic format that will enable team members to reflect on their roles within the broader organization. To give the team members the opportunity to create an action plan for developing objectives that align with the organization's goals and mission.
14. Astrodome Rescue	2	Structured Problem Solving	To give the team members the opportunity to examine the impact of personal values and attitudes on decision making. To give the team members the opportunity to study decision-making processes in groups. To give the team members the opportunity to practice consensus-seeking behavior.
15. The New Zin Obelisk	1	Structured Problem Solving	To give the team members the opportunity to experience and examine the sharing of information in team problem solving. To give the team members the opportunity to study leadership, cooperation, and other issues in team problem solving.
16. Role Negotiation	F, 2	Role Clarity	To provide the team members with a structured means of giving task-oriented feedback to one another. To help the team members to work through difficulties in personal and professional relationships.

ACTIVITY	RATING	USE WITH TEAM BLOCKAGE	GOALS
17. Airplane	1	Role Clarity	To give the team members the opportunity to examine the impact of roles in a team. To develop the members' skills in allocating roles in a team and in distributing the team's work among its members.
18. Giving Feedback	F, 1	Critique	To help the team to establish guidelines for giving feedback so that doing so becomes part of the team's culture. To increase the members' awareness of the importance of developing a team culture that values the giving and receiving of effective feedback. To give the team members the opportunity to develop their skills in giving and receiving feedback.
19. Pluses and Minuses	F, 3	Critique	To identify the strengths and weaknesses of a team's performance over a specified period. To give the team members the opportunity to reach consensus on ways that they can reinforce the positive aspects and overcome the negative aspects of their team's performance.
20. People-Skills Inventory	F, 2	Individual Development	To provide the team members with a systematic basis for self-evaluation and for team feedback on individual management skills. To identify team members' priorities for the development of management skills.
21. Good Coaching Practice	1	Individual Development	To give the team members the opportunity to identify and practice the skills involved in coaching. To help the team members to develop a "coaching climate."

ACTIVITY	RATING	USE WITH TEAM BLOCKAGE	GOALS
22. Team Brainstorming	1	Creativity	To give the team members the opportunity to practice a proven method of generating creative ideas. To develop the members' skills in creative problem solving. To improve the effectiveness of team meetings.
23. Creative Attitudes	1	Creativity	To give the team members the opportunity to explore attitudes that help or hinder the expression of creative ideas. To improve the creativity of team meetings.
24. Castles in the Air	1	Intergroup	To give the team members the opportunity to clarify the processes that are essential for the achievement of creative tasks. To give the members the opportunity to explore the dynamics of interteam relationships.
25. Interteam Mapping	1	Intergroup	To give the team members the opportunity to define their team's position within the broader organization. To give the members the opportunity to explore the nature of defined organizational relationships.

Setting Team-Building Objectives

Goals

    I. To clarify a team's development needs.

    II. To set objectives for team development and to establish criteria for measuring success.

    III. To provide a framework for beginning a team-building program.

Time Required

    Approximately two hours.

Materials

    I. A copy of the Team-Review Survey[1] and the Team-Building Work Sheet for each team member.

    II. A newsprint flip chart and a felt-tipped marker.

    III. Blank paper and a pencil for each team member.

Process

    I. The facilitator distributes the Team-Review Survey, the Team-Building Work Sheet, blank paper, and a pencil to each team member.

    II. Team members are directed to read the instructions and to complete the survey.

    III. After the team members have completed the Team-Review Survey, each member is instructed to write the names of the three blockages that he or she believes are most critical to the team's success on the Team-Review Interpretation Sheet (in the Team-Review Survey booklet).

---

[1] The Team-Review Survey is available from the Pfeiffer & Company office from which you purchased this book.

IV. At this point, the facilitator asks the team members whether they wish to express any concerns about the likely outcomes of openly discussing the survey results. The facilitator posts all members' concerns on the newsprint flip chart and discusses these concerns with the team members until they voluntarily express a willingness to proceed. Should anxieties remain, we suggest that the leader close the session and call in an external consultant to help the team proceed.

V. Following the team's agreement to proceed, the lists of blockages (from Step III) are submitted to the team's leader (this may be done anonymously).

VI. The leader posts the scores (see the Team-Review Survey Interpretation Sheet) and leads a discussion of the scores using the following questions:

1. How accurately do the survey results mirror our team's current position?

2. Is it important that we spend time on developing our team in the near future?

VII. At an appropriate point in the discussion, the facilitator gives the team members the task of reaching consensus on which blockages they want to resolve within the next three months.

VIII. After consensus has been achieved, the team members are asked to spend a few minutes to complete the Team-Building Work Sheet individually.

IX. Each member's contributions to the questions on the Team-Building Work Sheet are charted (anonymously, if preferred) and discussed. After reviewing all members' success criteria, the team agrees on a list of criteria and measurable objectives. If there is any difficulty in clarifying objectives or methods of tackling agreed-on objectives, the team can use the why/how approach described in Chapter 16.

X. The team then takes each item and brainstorms a suggested program for working on the chosen blockages. (Activity 22, "Team Brainstorming," provides a suitable structure for this process). This program can be developed further by the team's leader following the meeting.

TEAM-BUILDING WORK SHEET

Instructions: Use the statements below to capture your ideas for developing more effective teamwork.

We will know that we are making progress in clearing our team blockages when the following things *are* happening:

We will know that we are making progress in clearing our team blockages when the following things *are not* happening:

Leadership-Functions Analysis

Goals

I. To help the team to understand how leadership functions currently are carried out in the team.

II. To determine the best ways of carrying out leadership functions in the team.

Time Required

A maximum of two hours. It may be worthwhile to repeat this activity periodically as the team develops maturity and becomes more flexible.

Materials

I. A copy of the Leadership-Functions Analysis Questionnaire and a pencil for each team member.

II. A newsprint flip chart and a felt-tipped marker.

Process

I. This project should be undertaken only with the voluntary agreement of all team members. A copy of the Leadership-Functions Analysis Questionnaire is circulated to the members a few days before the planned session with a covering note asking whether people have any reservations. When voluntary participation has been affirmed, the facilitator may proceed with the activity.

II. Each team member, including the team leader, should complete the Leadership-Functions Analysis Questionnaire before the team meeting or at the beginning of the meeting.

III. The facilitator charts each item on the Leadership-Functions Analysis Questionnaire separately and tallies the individual responses. If any member has reservations about sharing his or her views with the group, all of the completed check sheets can be submitted anonymously.

IV. The team discusses each item, concentrating on areas that seem to require some change in methods of work or behavior. When the discussion is completed, the facilitator posts the suggested changes and leads the team in a review of the items until the members have reached consensus.

LEADERSHIP-FUNCTIONS ANALYSIS QUESTIONNAIRE

Instructions: Leadership functions are vital but are not always exercised by the team's formal leader. The Leadership-Functions Analysis Questionnaire helps those who play a role in the team's leadership to assess their current competence and to plan ways to improve.

Read each item carefully and circle the number that corresponds to your perception of how well you believe that leadership function is currently performed.

1. Encouraging contributions from all team members

1	2	3	4	5	6	7	8	9	10

performed to little
or no extent

performed to a
great extent

2. Ensuring that the team makes decisions

1	2	3	4	5	6	7	8	9	10

performed to little
or no extent

performed to a
great extent

3. Ensuring that objectives are set for each meeting

1	2	3	4	5	6	7	8	9	10

performed to little
or no extent

performed to a
great extent

4. Ensuring that team members work together effectively by adopting a logical and systematic approach to problem solving

1	2	3	4	5	6	7	8	9	10

performed to little
or no extent

performed to a
great extent

5. Putting energy into the team to start it off or to help it when it seems stuck

1	2	3	4	5	6	7	8	9	10

performed to little
or no extent

performed to a
great extent

6. Finding and bringing in external information to help the team's work stay relevant

| 1 | 2 | 3 | 4 | 5 | 6 | 7 | 8 | 9 | 10 |

performed to little
or no extent

performed to a
great extent

7. Representing the team effectively to other groups or teams

| 1 | 2 | 3 | 4 | 5 | 6 | 7 | 8 | 9 | 10 |

performed to little
or no extent

performed to a
great extent

8. Summarizing and clarifying discussions

| 1 | 2 | 3 | 4 | 5 | 6 | 7 | 8 | 9 | 10 |

performed to little
or no extent

performed to a
great extent

9. Supporting team members in difficult situations

| 1 | 2 | 3 | 4 | 5 | 6 | 7 | 8 | 9 | 10 |

performed to little
or no extent

performed to a
great extent

10. Energizing the team to be strengthened, not weakened, by problems

| 1 | 2 | 3 | 4 | 5 | 6 | 7 | 8 | 9 | 10 |

performed to little
or no extent

performed to a
great extent

11. Communicating a belief that a better future can be built

| 1 | 2 | 3 | 4 | 5 | 6 | 7 | 8 | 9 | 10 |

performed to little
or no extent

performed to a
great extent

12. Being able to stand back emotionally from difficulties

| 1 | 2 | 3 | 4 | 5 | 6 | 7 | 8 | 9 | 10 |

performed to little
or no extent

performed to a
great extent

13. Encouraging the expression of feelings and intuition

| 1 | 2 | 3 | 4 | 5 | 6 | 7 | 8 | 9 | 10 |

performed to little
or no extent

performed to a
great extent

14. Breaking tasks into smaller, more manageable components

| 1 | 2 | 3 | 4 | 5 | 6 | 7 | 8 | 9 | 10 |

performed to little
or no extent

performed to a
great extent

15. Taking time to review; learning from both successes and failures

| 1 | 2 | 3 | 4 | 5 | 6 | 7 | 8 | 9 | 10 |

performed to little
or no extent

performed to a
great extent

The Leadership-Style Profile

Goals

    I. To clarify the team leader's leadership style.

    II. To give team members the opportunity to give feedback to their team leader.

    III. To help the team leader plan how to build on his or her leadership strengths and to address any desired leadership improvements.

Time Required

    One and one-half hours.

Materials

    I. A copy of the Leadership-Style Profile and the Leadership-Style Profile Record Sheet for each team member.

    II. A pencil for each team member.

    III. A newsprint flip chart and a felt-tipped marker.

    IV. Masking tape for posting newsprint.

Process

    Open discussion of a team leader's style is difficult for both the leader and the team members and must be undertaken with sensitivity. It is essential that all team members voluntarily agree to participate before this activity is undertaken. Team members may prefer to keep their evaluations of their leader anonymous.

    I. The facilitator distributes a copy of the Leadership-Style Profile to each team member (this may be done a few days prior to the session) and invites each person to complete the Leadership-Style Profile Record Sheet (anonymously, if preferred). (Twenty minutes.)

    II. The facilitator creates a newsprint poster that will be used in analyzing the results of the Leadership-Style Profile Record Sheets. The poster will be used to display the leader's self-evaluation and to record the team members' ratings of the team leader. The poster should list the following items:

EXCEPTIONAL   "MORE OF"   "LESS OF" SUGGESTIONS FOR
   ITEMS   ITEMS   ITEMS   IMPROVEMENT

(Five minutes.)

III. The team members are instructed to discuss each item of the Leadership-Style Profile in order to clarify their reasons for responding as they did. The facilitator may ask the members to give the leader specific examples of his or her behaviors if the members feel comfortable doing so. (Fifteen minutes.)

IV. The facilitator instructs the team members to suggest ways in which the leader could improve and lists all suggestions in the appropriate column on the newsprint poster. The facilitator emphasizes to the members that the purpose of the activity is *not* to pressure the leader to change his or her behavior. Rather, the activity is a preliminary exploration of the leader's behaviors and the team members' feelings about these behaviors. (Fifty minutes.)

LEADERSHIP-STYLE PROFILE

Instructions: Read through each of the leadership-behavior items below. Please give your candid opinion of the leader of this team by identifying five items that you believe this leader performs exceptionally well. Mark these with the number *1.*

Next, identify five items that you would like this leader to do more of. Mark these with the number *2.*

Finally, identify five items (or fewer if you cannot find five) that you would like this leader to do less of. Mark these with the number *3.*

LEADERSHIP-BEHAVIOR ITEMS

_____ 1. Delegates in order to develop people

_____ 2. Carefully collects ideas and contributions from all team members

_____ 3. "Sells" ideas to people in the team to justify his or her views

_____ 4. Involves team members in all key decisions

_____ 5. Encourages the full contribution of all team members

_____ 6. Gains support through demonstrating strong personal commitment

_____ 7. Allows team members to operate autonomously

_____ 8. Is consistent

_____ 9. Has analyzed his or her role clearly

_____ 10. Is accountable for the work of the team

_____ 11. Encourages team members' creativity

_____ 12. Takes risks

_____ 13. Encourages team members to give feedback on his or her leadership style

_____ 14. Looks for learning opportunities for the team

_____ 15. Is psychologically distant from the team

_____ 16. Behaves consistently

_____ 17. Clarifies what team members expect and need from one another

_____ 18. Accepts leadership initiatives by other team members

_____ 19. Ensures that all team members are certain about their roles in relation to the team

_____ 20. Makes decisions without talking them through with the team

_____ 21. Adapts his or her style to changing circumstances

_____ 22. Is sensitive to the different needs of each team member

_____ 23. Competently represents the team at higher levels in the organization

_____ 24. Demonstrates deeply held beliefs about what is good and bad, important and unimportant

_____ 25. Ensures that team aims and objectives are clearly understood by all concerned

_____ 26. Directs the team's effort toward achievement by monitoring members' performance

_____ 27. Identifies team members' needs and gives practical help

_____ 28. Works at being a useful resource to others in problem solving

_____ 29. Talks about a desirable future that offers better ways of doing things or of redressing wrongs

_____ 30. Is persuasive in argument and debate

_____ 31. Builds a logical case and presents sound arguments

_____ 32. Uses his or her influence to cajole, demand, insist, or push people to act differently

_____ 33. Has well-developed skills in organizational design, planning, performance control, and administration

_____ 34. Exposes people to new ideas, experiences, concepts, possibilities, or inner reflections

_____ 35. Encourages and empowers people to take initiatives

_____ 36. Is deeply aware of the impact of his or her leadership style on others

_____ 37. Is authentic—says what he or she really means

_____ 38. Exercises discipline over team members

_____ 39. Shows deep commitment to all members of the team

_____ 40. Is committed to the possibility of continuous improvement

LEADERSHIP-STYLE PROFILE RECORD SHEET

Your Name (optional):_____

Instructions: Record the numbers of the items that you selected in the appropriate columns below.

Five items that you believe this leader performs exceptionally well	Five items that you would like this leader to do more of	Five items (or fewer) that you would like this leader to do less of

Activity 4

Team-Roles Analysis Questionnaire[1]

Goals

   I. To give the team members an opportunity to discuss the different ways that people contribute to teams.

   II. To foster the team members' respect for one another's differences.

   III. To help the team members to find ways to enhance their contributions to the team.

Time Required

One hour and fifteen minutes.

Materials

   I. A copy of the Team-Roles Analysis Questionnaire, the Team-Roles Analysis Questionnaire Scoring Sheet, and the Team-Roles Analysis Questionnaire Interpretation Sheet for each team member.

   II. A pencil for each team member.

   III. A newsprint flip chart and a felt-tipped marker.

   IV. Masking tape for posting newsprint.

Process

   I. The facilitator distributes the Team-Roles Analysis Questionnaire and invites each team member to complete it according to the directions on the instrument. (Fifteen minutes.)

---

[1] The authors acknowledge that some of the ideas in this activity and the questionnaire design are based on research conducted by Meredith Belbin at the Henley Management College, England, the findings of which were published in his book *Management Teams: Why They Succeed or Fail,* London: Heinemann, 1982. The definitions of team roles are partly based on the Myers-Briggs Type Inventory model, and the skill definitions were drawn from *Effective Problem Solving* by Dave Francis, London: Routledge, 1990.

II. The facilitator distributes copies of the Team-Roles Analysis Questionnaire Scoring Sheet to the team members and invites them to complete their sheets according to the directions. (Five minutes.)

III. The facilitator distributes copies of the Team-Roles Analysis Questionnaire Interpretation Sheet and asks the team members to read their handouts. (Five minutes.)

IV. The facilitator instructs the members to discuss their scores and their reactions to the Team-Roles Analysis Questionnaire Interpretation Sheet. (Subgroups of two to three members may be formed for this step if desired.) The facilitator asks the team members to answer the following questions:

1. What is each member's dominant team role(s)? How could each member's role(s) be developed further?

2. What roles does each member possess to a lesser extent? Should these roles be developed further? If so, how?

3. (If this team is being assessed) What are this team's dominant roles? In what ways do these roles strengthen the team?

4. (If this team is being assessed) What roles does this team practice to a lesser extent or not at all? In what ways might the absence of these roles weaken the team? How could this team begin to play these roles or strengthen its ability to do so?

(Forty minutes.)

IV. In a team meeting, the facilitator asks the members to brainstorm suggestions for improving their contributions to the team and lists them on a flip chart. (Fifteen minutes.)

Variation

The Team-Roles Analysis Questionnaire may also be used for training purposes, for teaching, or in workshops on skill development in teams.

TEAM-ROLES ANALYSIS QUESTIONNAIRE

Instructions: This questionnaire will help you to clarify how you operate in teams and will give you the opportunity to consider whether you wish to modify your team behavior.

The questionnaire has five sections, each of which focuses on a different team behavior. For each section, you will be asked to allocate ten points. The number of points that you assign to each statement should reflect your perception of your behavior at the present time. The more strongly that you believe you demonstrate a particular behavior, the more points you should allocate to that item. *Be sure to allocate ten points **only**—no more, no less—to each section.*

Before you complete the Team-Roles Analysis Questionnaire, decide whether you wish to consider your team-based behavior in general or you wish to focus on your behavior in a particular team. You may choose either approach, but be sure to respond consistently in light of the approach that you choose. Take a moment now to choose your focus and to mark the appropriate statement below.

_____ I am reviewing my behavior in this team.

_____ I am reviewing my behavior in teams in general.

Please respond to each item in every section.

SECTION ONE: DECISION MAKING

When a decision is being made in my team, I...

POINTS

1. State my opinion as a specialist in my own discipline

2. Explore the full implications of all ideas suggested

3. Take an independent viewpoint by considering every aspect

4. Evaluate the impact of possible decisions on other groups

5. Persuade the team to accept my point of view

6. Foster an atmosphere of openness in the team so that people can say what they really think

7. Offer radical suggestions that no one else has considered

8. Structure the discussion so that each member clearly understands the available options

9. Make sure that the team adheres to a strict timetable for decision making

10. Help the other team members to clarify their views

SECTION TWO: CREATIVITY

In a team brainstorming or creativity session, I...

11. Can be relied on to come up with unexpected ideas

12. Stand back and comment on what others say

13. Quickly choose the best idea and encourage others to adopt my viewpoint

14. Contribute to the session if I believe that I can add something of value

15. Organize the team so that the brainstorming process is executed properly

16. Build on the ideas of others

17. Contribute ideas that are relevant to my professional or technical training

18. Create the right climate for a productive, creative session

19. Bring in ideas from outside the team

20. Make sure that the team maintains a strict schedule so that the session is productive

SECTION THREE: PLANNING

When the team is planning what needs to be done, I...

POINTS

21. Assign actions and priorities to others

22. Consider the possible implications of our plans on other teams

23. Make sure that effective planning methods are used

24. Pull together proposals and develop comprehensive plans

25. Contribute ideas pertaining to those subjects in which I have expertise

26. Make sure that a clear timetable for action is developed

27. Help to motivate my team members

28. Assist the team in whatever ways seem helpful

29. Consider each aspect of the plan to ensure that it is realistic

30. Invent unexpected ways to use resources

SECTION FOUR: TEAM EFFECTIVENESS

When the team is reviewing its effectiveness, I...

POINTS

31. Make sure that the views of each
team member are considered

32. Present my opinions and ideas when
they would be helpful

33. Get the opinions of people outside
the team

34. Question the fundamental
effectiveness of the team and
suggest radical changes

35. Summarize every viewpoint and
evaluate the team's overall
strengths and weaknesses

36. Contribute as a functional specialist

37. Record all of the useful points
and establish a timetable for
improvement

38. Take an impartial attitude in
order to evaluate the team objectively

39. Decide what needs to be done and
convince others to accept my views

40. Stimulate open communication
among team members

SECTION FIVE: VALUING CONTRIBUTIONS

Others value my work in teams because...

POINTS

41. I work hard to create a positive climate

42. I think of innovative ideas

43. I am flexible

44. I contribute specialized knowledge and expertise

45. I make sure that things get done

46. I build positive links with other teams

47. I bring structure to team meetings

48. I provide leadership

49. I build on other people's ideas

50. I provide an impartial assessment of the team's activities

TEAM-ROLES ANALYSIS QUESTIONNAIRE SCORING SHEET

Instructions: Transfer your scores from the questionnaire items to the appropriate blanks below. Then add the items in each horizontal row of scores and record your total in the blank box provided.

Item Number					Your Totals	Team Roles
8	15	23	31	47		Process Manager
2	16	24	35	19		Concept Developer
7	11	30	34	42		Radical
6	18	27	40	41		Harmonizer
1	17	25	36	44		Technical Expert
9	20	26	37	45		Output Driver
3	12	29	38	50		Critic
10	14	28	32	43		Cooperator
5	13	21	39	48		Politician
4	19	22	33	46		Promoter

TEAM-ROLES ANALYSIS QUESTIONNAIRE
INTERPRETATION SHEET

PROCESS MANAGER

Process management comprises a set of skills that should be acquired by all leaders of teams. The process manager channels human resources to get things done. He or she forms teams, identifies team members' strengths, clarifies objectives, structures meetings, explores issues, allocates roles, and maintains momentum. The process manager brings structure to the team and ensures that goals are set. He or she has the skills of a good chairperson: control, self-confidence, calmness, and the ability to communicate well with others.

CONCEPT DEVELOPER

The concept developer ensures that ideas are developed and evaluated. This person helps to identify possibilities and transform them into practical proposals. The concept developer has the ability to see the potential merits and drawbacks of ideas. When someone suggests an idea, the concept developer will elaborate on it so that it can be assessed. The concept developer is creative and excels in envisioning, imagining, thinking logically, and understanding.

RADICAL

The radical presents new ideas by considering problems and opportunities from unexplored angles. This person sees new possibilities, adopts unconventional approaches, has insights, and produces novel proposals. The radical often is strongly intuitive. Radicals look at situations with a fresh perspective, prefer to think things through independently, and refuse to accept "conventional wisdom." The radical is a free spirit.

HARMONIZER

The harmonizer builds team morale by energizing, supporting, and encouraging others and by resolving interpersonal conflicts. The harmonizer believes that team efficiency is based on positive interpersonal relationships. He or she encourages commitment and cooperation and, thereby, good performance. The predominant impression that others have of the harmonizer is that he or she is a caring person. The harmonizer tries to ensure that team members value one another and gain something significant from their membership in the team.

TECHNICAL EXPERT

The technical expert is a subject-matter specialist. The technical expert contributes an expert or professional viewpoint to the team, making the team the beneficiary of his or her extensive training and experience in a particular area.

OUTPUT DRIVER

The output driver makes sure that tasks are completed. He or she sets time limits and targets and follows through on assignments. The output driver pushes to get things done and maintains standards. He or she checks to see whether things could go wrong at the last minute and is a creative tactician and planner.

CRITIC

The team member who takes the role of the critic must be intellectually capable, temperamentally inclined, and appropriately skilled. The critic takes a mental step back from the team to judge, to consider possibilities, to look for possible pitfalls, to sound notes of caution, and to question and challenge ideas. He or she confronts the team with objective observations and carefully weighed opinions. The critic's commentary should be objective, not negative or positive.

COOPERATOR

The cooperator is an industrious team member who assists in whatever ways are needed by working hard and by being adaptable. The cooperator is sensitive to others' needs and is willing to tackle unpleasant jobs without complaint. To succeed as a cooperator, a person must have well-developed observation skills, a sense of altruism, enthusiasm, and a variety of capabilities. The cooperator's key contribution to the team is flexibility.

POLITICIAN

Because politicians believe that they know the right thing to do, they try to influence other people to support their opinions. They mold the team's views, build alliances, and guide others. Politicians are results oriented, influential, power conscious, and persuasive. Such people are dogged and resolute; they bounce back after setbacks. The role of politician has been described as that of a "shaper," as the politician shapes opinions and objectives.

PROMOTER

The promoter is an extrovert with a set of appropriate skills. The promoter gathers useful contacts and makes connections outside the team. He or she is open minded, socially skilled, and cooperative. This person links the team to others with his or her outgoing and sociable nature and ability to build relationships, to investigate resources, and to check out ideas and possibilities. Promoters are "fixers" who enable things to get done.

Use Us—We're the Best

Goals

   I. To critically review the skills, capabilities, and potential of a team.

   II. To evaluate the marketability of a team.

Time Required

   Approximately one hour and forty-five minutes.

Materials

   I. A copy of the Use Us—We're the Best Task Sheet for each team member.

   II. An audiotape recorder *or* a video camera, a videocassette recorder (VCR), and a monitor.

   III. Blank paper and a pencil for each team member.

   IV. A newsprint flip chart and felt-tipped markers.

Process

   I. The facilitator distributes the Use Us—We're the Best Task Sheets, paper, and pencils to the team members and provides the team with a newsprint flip chart and felt-tipped markers.

   II. The facilitator instructs the team members to read the sheets and to complete the task described on the Task Sheets. (One hour.)

   III. At the end of the allotted time, the team members may be asked to share their results with other teams in the organization and to solicit their feedback. (Fifteen minutes.)

   IV. At this point, the team's leader should join the team members (even if he or she is acting as facilitator) to discuss what the members have learned from the activity and what skills the members believe need to be developed or enhanced. It is recommended that the leader list and retain the conclusions. (Thirty minutes.)

USE US—WE'RE THE BEST TASK SHEET

The Situation

Yesterday the leader of your team was told the following by the company's top management:

"We're sorry to have to say this, but we have reached a critical point and it is questionable whether this company can survive. As you know, we are a decent organization and have never fired people unless it was absolutely necessary. The way things are, we see two alternatives for your team. We could close the team down immediately, or you could market the team's services outside this company. If you choose to do the latter, you will be required to cover more than 50 percent of your costs. We know that the market is tough and the competition is strong, but we think that you can succeed. You have excellent people on your team, and you can hire some additional people if you want to, provided you cover the costs. You have six months to plan and prepare for the launch."

Your Team's Task

Your team must immediately assist your leader in this crisis. Working as a team, you have one hour to do the following:

1. Identify your team's skills and capabilities that would be useful to other organizations.
2. Identify any shortcomings that your team may have and any additional skills that your team needs; you are recommending that people with these skills be hired.
3. Decide what you will do to enhance the skills that your team already possesses. (Remember that your team is allowed six months of intensive effort to prepare.)
4. Prepare a brochure or, if the equipment is available, a radio or television commercial to advertise your new team and its services to potential customers.

Team-Development Stages

Goals

    I. To enable a team to evaluate its current stage of development.

    II. To offer the team members the opportunity to set priorities for the team's development.

    III. To help team members to evaluate their levels of commitment to the development of the team.

Time Required

    Forty-five minutes to one hour.

Materials

    I. A copy of the Team-Development Stages Theory Sheet and The Team-Development Clock for each team member.

    II. A pencil for each team member.

    III. A newsprint flip chart and a felt-tipped marker.

Process

    I. The facilitator distributes copies of the Team-Development Stages Theory Sheet and The Team-Development Clock and pencils to the team members and asks that each person read the descriptions of the five stages of team development. (Five minutes.)

    II. The facilitator instructs the team members to agree on a description of the team being studied. The facilitator then instructs each member to work *alone* to identify the stage that he or she believes most closely reflects the identified team's current stage of development. Each member then is asked to place a mark (such as an X) on The Team-Development Clock to represent this stage of development. (Fifteen minutes.)

    III. The facilitator draws a team-development clock on the newsprint flip chart, asks the team members to report their evaluation scores, and records the scores on the clock. (Five minutes.)

IV. The facilitator leads the team members in a discussion of their evaluations. It is helpful for the facilitator to ask each team member to clarify his or her views on the team's stage of development. If possible, specific examples of illustrative behaviors should be cited.

V. The facilitator asks the team members to reach consensus on their team's current level of development and helps the members to choose activities that will help to develop the team.

TEAM-DEVELOPMENT STAGES THEORY SHEET

Instructions: Working with the other members of your team, write a short description of the team that you are going to study in the box below.

The team to be studied is...

Stages of Team Development[1]

Stage 1: Testing. The group is not yet a true team; rather, it is a collection of individuals who share tasks. Relationships are polite, impersonal, guarded, and mannerly—in short, underdeveloped. Members are driven by self-interest. The members have not yet learned to think as a team. If the team manages to function effectively, it is because the members are doing a good job at playing their roles. Members are watchful of one another; the testing stage has been called the "ritual-sniffing" stage.

Stage 2: Infighting. The team members are beginning to coalesce. Members are sorting out their relationships with one another. During this stage, members may be argumentative and undisciplined, may not listen well, and may confront authority figures. Cliques and alliances may emerge. The infighting stage produces psychological involvement but little real commitment. Much energy is inner directed.

Stage 3: Learning. The team is willing to learn and to adopt a structured approach to problem solving and decision making. Team and individual effectiveness is reviewed. Members become more committed to one another as each person decides to "opt in." The team becomes focused on the tasks to be performed. It experiments with working methods and evaluates its performance.

---

[1] See also Tuckman & Jensen, 1977.

Stage 4: Performing. The team finally has learned to function effectively. The climate in the team is one of resourcefulness, confidence, openness, and flexibility. Meetings are efficient, roles are clarified, relationships are supportive but demanding, and energy is invested in tasks. Team members help one another and feel a sense of genuine warmth and affection. The team is open to others' ideas.

Stage 5: Declining. At this point, the team enters into a period of decline. Energy is lost; often, the team becomes inner focused and self-satisfied. Team members have become accustomed to turning to others for confirmation of their views. Ideas are not challenged. During this stage, members who criticize the status quo may be isolated or rejected.

REFERENCE

Tuckman, B.W., & Jensen, M.A.C. (1977, December). Stages of small-group development revisited. *Group & Organization Studies, 2*(4), 419-427.

THE TEAM-DEVELOPMENT CLOCK

Instructions: Place an X on the circle to indicate your perception of the current stage of development of the team being studied.

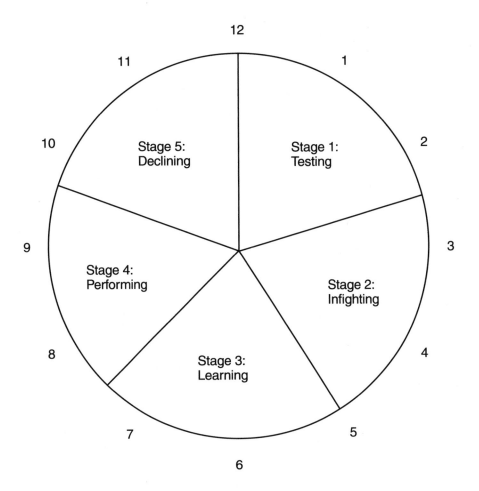

Designing a
Team-Building Workshop

Goals

I. To allow the team members to participate in defining the objectives and content of a planned team-building workshop.

II. To plan the team-building workshop so that it will utilize the members' time most efficiently.

Time Required

Two hours and fifteen minutes for the two team meetings, excluding subgroup work.

Materials

I. A pad of large Post-It™ notes for each team member.

II. A pencil for each team member.

III. A newsprint flip chart and a felt-tipped marker.

Physical Setting

A room that is large enough to accommodate the entire team, with enough space (or separate rooms) so that subgroups can work without disturbing one another.

Process

Part 1

I. The facilitator distributes a pad of Post-It™ notes and a pencil to each team member. He or she invites each member to identify three problems or opportunities that confront the team at this time and to write each legibly on a separate Post-It™ note. (Five minutes.)

II. The facilitator collects the Post-It™ notes, arranges them into categories by subject or theme, and posts the categories on newsprint. (Ten minutes.)

III. The facilitator instructs the team to look for any categories that seem significant and to estimate the importance of each issue by assigning priorities using the following key:

3 = Crucial
2 = Important
1 = Somewhat important
0 = Insignificant

(Fifteen minutes.)

IV. The team is asked to consider the degree of complexity inherent in each identified issue and to estimate the approximate amount of time that it will take to solve each problem. As the members discuss each issue, they should assign a time-factor number to each problem using the following scale:

4 = Very complex (more than one day to resolve)
3 = Complex (between two hours and one-half day to resolve)
2 = Straightforward (between one and two hours to resolve)
1 = Simple (less than one hour to resolve)

(Fifteen minutes.)

V. The facilitator copies the following headings onto the newsprint flip chart:

PROBLEM   IMPORTANCE   COMPLEXITY   TOTAL

The facilitator then lists the scores for each category on the flip chart and totals the scores. (Ten minutes.)

VI. Using the table that was created in Step V, the team determines the amount of time that it wishes to spend on its team-building workshop. The facilitator may wish to note to the team members that the value of a team-building workshop to participants generally doubles with each additional day (up to three days). (Ten minutes.)

VII. The facilitator divides the team members into dyads or triads and gives each subgroup the task of reviewing the activities in *Improving Work Groups* (and any other available materials) and designing a team-building workshop. The subgroups are invited to report back to the entire team in a few days' time. (Ten minutes.)

Part 2

I. After the subgroups have completed the assignment from Part 1, Step VII, the facilitator reconvenes the entire team.

II. Each subgroup presents its planned team-building session and its rationale for designing the session as it did. (Thirty minutes.)

III. The entire team discusses each plan. The team may choose one subgroup's approach or synthesize several subgroups' ideas into one workshop design. (Twenty-five minutes.)

IV. One person is appointed to arrange the team-building session. This person will be responsible for taking care of practical concerns, ensuring that materials are available, and coordinating the projects. (Five minutes.)

V. If the team feels too inexperienced to handle the team-building workshop on its own, it may wish to engage the services of an external consultant. (See Chapter 4, "Facilitating the Team-Building Process.")

Variation

This activity can be adapted to become the initial session in a team-building workshop. In this case, subgroups should be given one hour in which to create their proposals.

The Team-Climate Questionnaire

Goal

To give the team the opportunity to examine its working climate and to prepare an action plan for improving it.

Time Required

One hour. (Teams often find it valuable to recheck the data by administering the questionnaire on later occasions.)

Materials

  I. A copy of the Team-Climate Questionnaire and the Team-Climate Questionnaire Summary Sheet for each team member.

 II. A pencil for each team member.

III. A newsprint flip chart and a felt-tipped marker.

Physical Setting

A quiet room that is free from interruptions.

Process

  I. The facilitator copies the content of the summary sheet onto newsprint. (This will be used in summarizing the results of the completed questionnaires.)

 II. The facilitator distributes a copy of the Team-Climate Questionnaire and a pencil to each team member.

III. Team members are asked to read the instructions and to complete the instrument. (Ten minutes.)

 IV. After the team members have completed the questionnaire, the facilitator asks whether they want to report their scores orally or whether they would prefer to write their scores on paper and turn them in anonymously. If one or more members of the team prefer anonymous feedback, the latter method should be used. The Team Climate Questionnaire Summary Sheet can be used for this purpose.

V. The facilitator collects the scores and posts them on the newsprint chart that he or she prepared for this purpose, displaying the range of scores and the mean score for each questionnaire item.

VI. The facilitator leads the team members in a discussion of the following:

- The arithmetic mean (average) scores for each questionnaire item and the range of scores;
- Whether the team would develop better if its behavior moved more to the left or right side of the scale on each item;
- The specific behaviors that relate to each of the questionnaire items; and
- The overall climate of the team and the members' ideas for improving it.

VII. The team members are asked to conclude the activity by setting an action plan, which should be recorded and distributed.

VIII. From time to time this activity should be repeated and the scores compared with those from earlier surveys.

TEAM-CLIMATE QUESTIONNAIRE

Instructions: Before you complete the questionnaire, work with your team members to create a definition of the team being assessed and complete the box below.

The team that is being reviewed is...

Please give your candid opinion of this team by rating its characteristics on the seven-point scale that follows each item. Circle the number on each scale that corresponds to your evaluation. Please give your opinion in each case, even if you are not certain.

1. Are the members of this team open in their relationships with others?

1	2	3	4	5	6	7

   Team members
   are open   Team members
                                                are guarded

2. Do members have "hidden agendas" (motives that they are unwilling to reveal)?

1	2	3	4	5	6	7

   No member has
   a hidden agenda   Some members have
                                             a hidden agenda

3. Are some topics taboo for discussion within the team?

1	2	3	4	5	6	7

   Every topic can be
   discussed   Some topics cannot
                                             be discussed

4. Does the team have traditions that prevent it from working effectively?

1	2	3	4	5	6	7

There are no
unhelpful traditions

There are unhelpful
traditions

5. Are the ideas of senior members considered to be law?

1	2	3	4	5	6	7

Senior members
are challenged

The ideas of senior
members are law

6. Are radical views expressed freely?

1	2	3	4	5	6	7

Radical views are
expressed freely

Radical views are
not expressed

7. Do team members collaborate with one another?

1	2	3	4	5	6	7

Team members collaborate
with one another

Team members pull
against one another

8. What happens when a person makes a mistake?

1	2	3	4	5	6	7

People learn
from mistakes

People are punished
for mistakes

9. Do more experienced members help members who are less experienced?

1	2	3	4	5	6	7

Inexperienced members
are helped

Inexperienced members
are not helped

10. Are difficult or uncomfortable issues worked through openly?

1	2	3	4	5	6	7

Difficult issues are
worked through

Difficult issues are
not worked through

11. Are conflicts between team members "swept under the carpet"?

| 1 | 2 | 3 | 4 | 5 | 6 | 7 |

Conflicts are confronted and resolved

Conflicts are "swept under the carpet"

12. Can team members openly disagree with the team leader?

| 1 | 2 | 3 | 4 | 5 | 6 | 7 |

Members can disagree openly

Members cannot disagree openly

13. Does the team devote much energy to becoming efficient in its use of time?

| 1 | 2 | 3 | 4 | 5 | 6 | 7 |

Much energy is devoted

Little energy is devoted

14. Do team members believe that they can try new things, risk failure, and still get support?

| 1 | 2 | 3 | 4 | 5 | 6 | 7 |

Support for risk taking

No support for risk taking

15. Does the team encourage people to develop themselves?

| 1 | 2 | 3 | 4 | 5 | 6 | 7 |

Support for self-developmnet

No support for self-development

16. Have team members worked through their own beliefs and values with others?

| 1 | 2 | 3 | 4 | 5 | 6 | 7 |

Values have been explored

Values have not been explored

17. Do team members put energy into the team's tasks?

1	2	3	4	5	6	7

High energy
for tasks

Low energy
for tasks

18. Does membership in the team stimulate and energize the members?

1	2	3	4	5	6	7

Team energizes
members

Team does not
energize members

19. Do the team members trust one another as people?

1	2	3	4	5	6	7

High trust

Low trust

20. Does the team maintain positive relationships with other teams?

1	2	3	4	5	6	7

Positive relationships
are maintained

Positive relationships
are not maintained

TEAM-CLIMATE QUESTIONNAIRE SUMMARY SHEET

ISSUES	INDIVIDUAL SCORES	TEAM SCORE
1. Openness		
2. Hidden Agendas		
3. Taboos		
4. Traditions		
5. Senior Members		
6. Radical Views		
7. Working Together		
8. Mistakes		
9. Helping		
10. Uncomfortable Issues		
11. Conflict		
12. Open Disagreement		
13. Time Management		
14. Risk Taking		
15. Self-Development		
16. Beliefs and Values		
17. Task Energy		
18. Team Membership		
19. Trust		
20. Other Teams		

Fong Construction: A Study in Teamwork

Goals

I. To give the team members the opportunity to explore the fundamental causes of ineffective teamwork.

II. To develop the team members' capacity to analyze their team's climate.

III. To give the team members the opportunity to explore the techniques of effective leadership.

IV. To give the team members the opportunity to critique their team's skills, capabilities, and potential.

Time Required

One hour and thirty to forty minutes.

Materials

I. A copy of the Fong Construction Situation Sheet and the Fong Construction Task Sheet for each team member.

II. A newsprint flip chart and a felt-tipped marker.

III. A video camcorder to record the role plays for later study (optional).

IV. Masking tape for posting newsprint.

Process

I. The facilitator distributes the Fong Construction Situation Sheets and the Fong Construction Task Sheets to the team members and asks them to read the instructions and to plan their role plays. If the number of team members is larger than the number of roles on the situation sheet, the facilitator instructs the extra members to observe the role play and to take notes based on the questions on the Fong Construction Task Sheet. (Forty-five minutes.)

II. The facilitator instructs the subgroups to role play their situations. The facilitator may videotape the role plays if he or she wishes. (Ten minutes.)

III. The facilitator reconvenes the team and leads a discussion of what the members have learned from this activity. Observers are asked to comment on what they saw. The facilitator posts the team's major conclusions on a sheet of newsprint. (Thirty minutes.)

Variation

To enhance the dramatic effect of the role plays, a "stage" with name plates of the members of the Fong Construction top-management team can be prepared.

FONG CONSTRUCTION SITUATION SHEET

The setting:

A strategic-planning meeting of the Fong Construction top-management team.

The team:

Terry Fong	Chief Executive
Pat Smith	Finance Director
Chris Jackson	Marketing Director
Dale Thompson	Operations Director
Kelly James	Development Director
Sandy Black	Personnel Director
Lee White	Administration Director

The content of the meeting:

Chris: This company is in serious trouble. We are far too concerned with the practical problems of construction. No one takes the marketing aspect seriously. If we were thinking about the market, we would position ourselves correctly; we wouldn't be taking on no-hope jobs like the Landmark Project, which is costing us millions.

Dale: Construction is a cyclical business. We are bound to suffer periods when things look bad, but over a ten-year period this is always a good business.

Lee: I have some major concerns about our systems of control. You mentioned the Landmark Project. I went past there the other day at eight o'clock at night, and the place was deserted; yet I have done an analysis of the overtime payments, and these clearly show that we are working 24 percent overtime on grades four and five and 19 percent overtime on—

Sandy: Is this relevant? Surely the most important thing is motivation. The fact of the matter is that the teams on the Landmark job are demotivated. They are late; everyone is throwing bricks at them; and yet, as I understand it, the major fault lies with the operations people, who miscalculated the depth needed for foundations piling and who started late.

Dale: I resent the slur from Sandy. But I will let it pass. As far as the foundations-piling work is concerned, it turned out that there was a pocket of gault clay just beneath the southwest end. My surveyors followed the procedures. What more do you want?

Chris: What does all of this have to do with marketing? Terry, I'd like you to intervene. Surely this meeting is not an argument about the location of pockets of gault clay.

Dale: That pocket of gault clay will mean that you won't get a bonus this year.

Sandy: If you had been more careful about the training of the key members of your geotechnical department, we might not be in this mess. When we went to business school, they told us that the concept of key success factors is important. The competence of the geotechnical department in a foundations business is the number-one success factor.

Dale: If you had let me recruit the person I wanted, I would have had the resources. The penny-pinching attitude that personnel takes is the major headache that we have. I wanted the best; I was told to get the best; but we won't pay.

Sandy: You may feel that it's okay to throw the whole payment structure into confusion whenever you like, just to get a job done, but I do not.

Dale: This business is all about getting the job done.

Chris: What does this have to do with marketing? Terry, again I ask you to intervene. I thought this meeting was supposed to be about our business performance.

Terry: Of course you all are right, but you are taking a narrow point of view. The job is important, but so is the integrity of the salary structure. I want to discuss our business positioning and fundamental strategy. Chris, please introduce the topic.

Lee: But first I am concerned about the management-information system. Do we really have sufficient information to make decisions about our fundamental strategy?

Chris: That's not the purpose of a management-information system. What we need is a marketing-information system.

Sandy: Isn't that your job, Chris?

Kelly: These interpersonal squabbles are going to drag us down. I agree that people should be free to say what they really feel in this group, but the sniping and bitching are completely unproductive. We simply won't get anything done unless we cooperate.

Chris: Let me begin by reflecting on the market. Increasingly, the market is being dominated either by major internationals, which I will call category-one players. Some of the category-one players are generalists; I'll call them the category-one-A players. Others are focus or segment specialists; I'll call them the category-one-B players. Of course, not all of the internationals fit into these categories because some are strong in several interrelated niches. Then there are the local players, who are either smaller versions of the internationals or who are geographically defined and gain competitive advantage from their locations.

Terry: Do you have any figures that are related to return on investment for each of these categories?

Chris: Yes. But I'll have to get them from my office.

Terry: Perhaps it's a good time to take a break.

FONG CONSTRUCTION TASK SHEET

Instructions: Read the Fong Construction Situation Sheet and analyze the strengths and weaknesses of the top-management team. After you have finished, you and your subgroup should prepare a role play, lasting no longer than seven minutes, to show how Terry Fong *should have* conducted the meeting. Subgroups with fewer than seven members should omit appropriate roles as needed. Listed below are some questions for you and your subgroup to consider in analyzing the situation sheet.

1. What is the climate in the team? Why has that climate emerged? What are the strengths and weaknesses of the climate?
2. To what extent is the apparent absence of good interpersonal relationships a factor in the top-management team's performance?
3. If you were Terry Fong, what would you do? How would you do it? What leadership style would be most likely to succeed with this group of people?
4. If you were a team-development consultant who was called in to help this team, what would you do? How?
5. To what extent do the top managers have a clear picture of the team's task and mission?
6. How can a team leader encourage a team to avoid partisan "special pleading" by some members in pursuit of their own interests?
7. What messages are being sent to the organization by this team's method of operating?

Activity 10

Charting Team Success

Goals

  I. To examine the team's recent achievements.

 II. To consider the forces (internal and external) that influence the success or failure of a team.

Time Required

One hour and fifteen minutes.

Materials

  I. A copy of the Team-Success Chart Task Sheet and the Team-Success Chart for each team member.

 II. Two pens, in different colors, for each team member.

III. A newsprint flip chart and a felt-tipped marker.

 IV. Masking tape for posting newsprint.

Process

  I. Before the meeting, the facilitator should reproduce the Team-Success Chart on a newsprint poster.

 II. The facilitator distributes a copy of the Team-Success Chart Task Sheet and the Team-Success Chart to each team member and explains the purpose of the chart. The facilitator then asks team members individually to draw two trend lines on the Team-Success Chart. The first line (in one color) is to represent that member's evaluation of the team's success; the second line (in another color) is to represent that member's perception of the team's morale in the past six months. The facilitator instructs the team members to annotate their lines as shown on the handout. (Fifteen minutes.)

III. The facilitator collects the completed Team-Success Charts and charts the individual trend lines on the Team-Success Chart that he or she prepared on newsprint. The facilitator then estimates the team's mean for each month and draws a line, perhaps in a different

227

color, on the Team-Success Chart to represent the overall team pattern.

IV. The facilitator leads the members in a discussion of the team's trend line and asks the members to think of reasons for any shifts in their perceptions of the levels of team success or morale. The facilitator records the members' comments on the appropriate locations of the newsprint Team-Success Chart. (Forty-five minutes.)

V. The team members are invited to reflect on their analysis and to identify areas in which the team can improve. The facilitator clarifies and records their ideas. (Fifteen minutes.)

TEAM-SUCCESS CHART TASK SHEET

Instructions: Study the sample Team-Success Chart below; then draw two trend lines on your blank Team-Success Chart. One line is to represent your evaluation of your team's success; the other line is to represent your perception of your team's morale in the past six months. Use two colors to distinguish your lines. When you have finished, annotate your lines as illustrated in the sample Team-Success Chart.

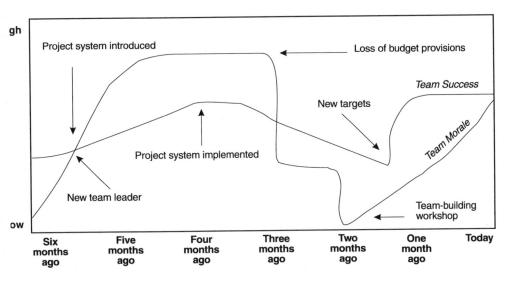

Sample Team-Success Chart

Your Team-Success Chart

A Brilliant Future

Goals

I. To explore any barriers toward team achievement that the members may recognize.

II. To motivate team members toward higher achievement.

Time Required

Two hours.

Materials

I. A copy of A Brilliant Future Task Sheet and A Brilliant Future Review Sheet for each team member.

II. A newsprint flip chart and a felt-tipped marker.

III. Masking tape for posting newsprint.

IV. A video camcorder and a monitor for playback.

Process

I. The facilitator (who, in this activity, should be the team's leader) introduces the exercise by explaining that the team is about to undertake a creative exercise that will stimulate the team members and that will help them to create their desired future. All team members should be encouraged to participate. The facilitator then distributes a copy of A Brilliant Future Task Sheet to each team member and joins the team as a full member. (Five minutes.)

II. As a team, the members read A Brilliant Future Task Sheet and complete the task as directed. (Eighty minutes.)

III. The finished video is shown to the team and to outside observers if the team desires. (Five minutes.)

IV. The facilitator distributes a copy of A Brilliant Future Review Sheet to each team member and leads the team in a review of the task as suggested. (Thirty minutes.)

231

A BRILLIANT FUTURE TASK SHEET

Instructions: Your team's task is to produce a short video that could be shown in a television program called "Superteams." Because of your team's fantastic progress and reputation for outstanding productivity, it has been selected to be featured in the television program.

Assume that "Superteams" will be produced in two years' time.

Use the following guidelines in producing your team's film:

1. The final film should be between three and five minutes in length.
2. The film should have a theme and should be structured as a "story" with a beginning, a middle, and an end.
3. All members of your team (except the camera operator) should have significant roles in the final film.
4. Follow the rules for good television: make the message clear and the delivery powerful.
5. In the film, mention at least five reasons for your team's fantastic progress and outstanding productivity.
6. A script is optional; contributors may ad lib if they wish.
7. Your team has eighty minutes in which to plan and produce the film.

A BRILLIANT FUTURE REVIEW SHEET

Think about the film that your team made and discuss the following questions as a team:

1. What did it feel like to work together to make the film?
2. Would you like to work in a team like the one that was portrayed in the film? Why or why not?
3. What prevents this team from becoming as effective as the team that was portrayed in the film?
4. What is each team member willing to contribute to the development of the team?
5. What is each team member *not* willing to contribute to the development of the team?
6. What practical steps toward self-development will your team take in the next month or two?

Team Survival

Goal

To give the team a method of justifying its existence to the broader organization.

Time Required

One hour and thirty minutes.

Materials

I. A copy of the Team Survival Task Sheet and the Team Survival Review Sheet for each participant.

II. A copy of the Team Survival Assessor's Briefing for each assessor.

III. A newsprint flip chart and a felt-tipped marker.

Process

I. The facilitator presents the team-survival task to the team members and answers any questions that the team members may have. (Full instructions are given in the Team Survival Task Sheet and in the Team Survival Assessor's Briefing.) If the team's leader is acting as the facilitator, he or she should join the team as a participant at this time. The team then undertakes the task as directed. (Fifty minutes.)

II. The team makes its presentation to at least one nonmember of the team, preferably someone with a forceful personality to enhance the realistic nature of the activity. The assessor(s) should be briefed about the objectives of the activity and should be given a copy of the Team Survival Assessor's Briefing before the presentation. (Ten minutes.)

III. The assessor(s) gives feedback to the team about its presentation. (Ten minutes.)

IV. The facilitator distributes a copy of the Team Survival Review Sheet to each team member and instructs the members to discuss the questions on the sheet. (Twenty minutes.)

TEAM SURVIVAL TASK SHEET

The Situation

A new chief executive officer (CEO) has just joined your organization. She is reputed to be a tough, hard-line decision maker. Her specialty has been the cutting of costs and staff, which has produced dramatic results in some of the companies in which she has worked.

It appears that the new CEO is a person of considerable energy and drive, single-minded in her determination to cut costs and to trim unnecessary staff. It is said that the only way to influence her is with strong, well-thought-out logic—after all, she already has shut down entire departments with little discussion. Rumors have been spreading that your team is the next one to be cut. It is now 10:10 a.m., and your boss has been summoned to an 11:00 a.m. meeting with the CEO, who wants a justification of your team's existence in the organization.

Your Team's Task

You have fifty minutes to help your team leader prepare a presentation for the CEO. Your leader must prove beyond question that your team is essential to the success of the organization. This presentation is critical: If your team's case is not strong enough, all of its members will be discharged from the organization.

In preparing the presentation, you should consider the following:

- The goals and strategies of the broader organization;
- Your team's contribution to the broader organization;
- The cost/benefit equation in keeping or dismissing the members of your team;
- The consequences that the organization would suffer if your team were disbanded; and
- The possible ramifications of massive cuts to your team's staffing budget.

TEAM SURVIVAL ASSESSOR'S BRIEFING

You are the new chief executive officer of this organization. You are preparing to hear a presentation from the leader of a team that you believe may be unnecessary to the success of the organization. You will listen to the team leader's presentation with an open mind, but the leader must convince you with substantiated data that the team is essential to the organization in order for you to retain it.

Listed below are some of the issues that you plan to consider while listening to the team leader's presentation:

1. Do I need additional data in order to make a judgment about the value of this team to the organization? What additional data are needed?
2. Am I convinced that this team is essential to the success of the organization as a whole? If not, what would it take to convince me?
3. What unique and essential contributions does this team make to the organization as a whole?
4. Do I want the team to improve its contribution to the organization? If so, in what specific areas?

After you have finished evaluating the team leader's presentation, give the team five minutes of feedback on its strengths and weaknesses as you see them.

TEAM SURVIVAL REVIEW SHEET

Reflect individually on the activity that you have completed and consider the questions below. With your team members, discuss the questions and reach consensus.

1. How clear are you about your team's role and contribution to the broader organization? In your own words, define your team's role and contribution.

2. What disagreements arose while you and your team members were preparing the presentation? Why do you think these disagreements arose?

3. What have you learned about your team's purpose within the broader organization?

4. Would it be useful to test the reactions of other teams to your definition of your team's role? How could this be done?

5. What actions could you take to improve your and your team's contribution to your organization?

Adding Value

Goals[1]

I. To give the team members an opportunity to explore the concepts of value, of the value chain, and of adding value.

II. To present a systematic format that will enable team members to reflect on their roles within the broader organization.

III. To give the team members the opportunity to create an action plan for developing objectives that align with the organization's goals and mission.

Time Required

Two hours.

Materials

I. A copy of the Adding Value Task Sheet for each team member.

II. A newsprint flip chart and a felt-tipped marker.

Process

I. The facilitator distributes the Adding Value Task Sheets to the team members, introduces the task outlined thereon, and answers any questions that the team members may have. If the team's leader is acting as the facilitator, he or she should join the team at this time. (Twenty minutes.)

II. The team completes the task as described on the Adding Value Task Sheet. (Forty minutes.)

III. The team presents its ideas to senior management and requests feedback. If necessary, the definition of "added value" can be amended after the meeting. (One hour.)

---

[1] This activity also may be used to promote positive interteam relationships (see blockage 12). The value-chain model was developed by Michael Porter and is described in his book, *Competitive Advantage,* New York: The Free Press, 1986.

ADDING VALUE TASK SHEET

Read the definition of "value added" and, as a team, answer the questions below. Prepare a presentation (as if to members of senior management) as suggested.

What is "Value Added"?

Each activity that an organization undertakes should (either directly or indirectly) add value. *Value* can be defined as something that customers are willing to pay for. Value is therefore determined by the customer, not by the organization's management.

The theory of *value chains* conceptualizes the organization as an interlinked system of value-adding activities that, like the sections of an orchestra, must operate in harmony. The value-chain theory classifies activities as either *direct* or *indirect,* as follows:

Direct Activities

Inbound logistics: obtaining raw materials

Operations: transforming raw materials into finished goods or useful services

Outbound logistics: moving finished goods to places where they can be sold, or supplying useful services

Sales and marketing: finding out what people want and persuading them to buy a particular product or service

Service: ensuring that customers receive enduring value from a product or service

Indirect Activities

Procurement: purchasing everything that is needed to operate the organization

Technology: using systems, methods, and techniques to control, coordinate, and set standards

Human resource development: recruiting, selecting, promoting, rewarding, training, and organizing employees

Infrastructure: the means by which organizational members secure funding, determine strategies, and manage the overall organization

As a team, discuss the following questions:

1. In which of the nine areas of activity described above does your team make its most significant contribution?

2. How would you describe the role that your team plays as it relates to the total organizational system of operations?
3. What activities does your team undertake that do not add value to the organization?
4. What additional activities could your team undertake that would add value to the organization? Why would these activities add value? How could your team implement them?
5. How efficient is the flow of information between your team and the other parts of the organization to which it adds value?

Your Team's Task

Prepare a presentation (if possible, to senior management) that:

- Explains how your team adds value to the organization;
- Explains in what ways your team *does not* add value to the organization; and
- Suggests ways that your team could add more value to the organization in the future.

Astrodome Rescue[1]

Goals

   I. To give the team members the opportunity to examine the impact of personal values and attitudes on decision making.

  II. To give the team members the opportunity to study decision-making processes in groups.

 III. To give the team members the opportunity to practice consensus-seeking behavior.

Group Size

Any number of subgroups of a team, each comprising four to seven members, may be directed simultaneously.

Time Required

One hour and thirty minutes.

Materials

   I. A copy of the Astrodome Rescue Briefing Sheet, the Astrodome Rescue Biography Sheet, and the Astrodome Rescue Review Sheet for each team member.

  II. A copy of the Astrodome Rescue Ranking Sheet for each team.

 III. A pencil for each team member.

 IV. A newsprint flip chart and a felt-tipped marker for each team.

Physical Setting

A room large enough to accommodate a circle of chairs for each team, with enough space between teams to allow some measure of privacy. Separate rooms, if available, may be used.

---

[1] The authors gratefully acknowledge the contribution of Mike Woodcock, co-author of the original version of this activity, "Cave Rescue."

Process

 I. The facilitator briefly explains the goals of the activity and states that, because some team members may not wish to take part for ethical reasons, participation must be completely voluntary.

 II. The facilitator divides the team members into equal-sized groups of four to seven members each. Each group should have privacy.

 III. The facilitator distributes the Astrodome Rescue Briefing Sheets, the Astrodome Rescue Biography Sheets, and pencils to the team members. The team members are instructed to read their sheets. (Five minutes.)

 IV. The facilitator distributes a copy of the Astrodome Rescue Ranking Sheet to each subgroup and directs each subgroup to discuss and complete its sheet. (Forty-five minutes.)

 V. The facilitator calls time, collects the ranking sheets, and distributes a copy of the Astrodome Rescue Review Sheet to each team member.

 VI. Working in their subgroups, the team members are instructed to complete the Astrodome Rescue Review Sheets and to share their responses with one another. (Thirty minutes.)

 VII. The facilitator reconvenes the entire team and leads the members in a discussion of the activity, focusing on the members' reactions to the questions on the Astrodome Rescue Review Sheet.

Variations

 I. Additional "volunteer" characters can be created for inclusion on the Astrodome Rescue Biography Sheet.

 II. Some subgroup members may be instructed to observe the group process and to share their observations with their groups during Step VI.

ASTRODOME RESCUE BRIEFING SHEET

Your group has been asked to take the role of a research-management committee, which is responsible for administering extraterrestrial research projects at the state university. You have been called to an emergency meeting because of a calamity in one of the projects for which the committee is responsible.

The project, which is studying likely human behavior in a colony to be established on another planet, is conducting an experiment in an astrodome in the Colorado desert. The experiment involves six volunteers, who are living in the astrodome for two weeks. The volunteers' only outside connection is a radio link to a research station. A call for help from the volunteers has been received; helium gas is escaping from the astrodome, which is reducing the oxygen level to a life-threatening extent.

The rescue team reports that rescue will be extremely difficult and, with the equipment that is available, only one person can be rescued every fifteen minutes. Therefore, it is possible that some of the volunteers will asphyxiate due to the rapidly dwindling oxygen supply before they can be rescued. Through their radio link with the research station, the volunteers have been made aware of the dangers of their plight. They have communicated that they are unwilling to decide on the sequence in which they are to be rescued. You, the research-management committee, now are responsible for deciding the order in which the volunteers are to be rescued.

Lifesaving equipment will arrive at the entrance to the astrodome in fifty minutes. At that time, you must provide the rescue team with the order in which you wish the volunteers to be rescued.

The only available information about the volunteers has been drawn from the project files and is reproduced on the Astrodome Rescue Biography Sheet. Use any criteria you wish to help you make your decisions. An Astrodome Rescue Ranking Sheet should be completed by your group and submitted within fifty minutes.

ASTRODOME RESCUE BIOGRAPHY SHEET

Volunteer 1: Mary. White female; American; age 31.

Mary is the project's cook. She is married; her husband is a factory worker in a dog-food plant. She had been a home-economics student before she left college to be married. Mary has four children (aged seven months to eight years) and lives in a run-down community near a train station. Her hobbies are running a children's play group and watching television. Mary became involved in the project through Jake, with whom she has become sexually involved.

Volunteer 2: John. Black male; American; age 43.

John is now married to his third wife. He is the campus coordinator of pastoral services at the state university. He has five children by his first and second wives. John supports the children, who range in age from six to nineteen years, and sees them on weekends. John worked full-time while attending the university and earned a master's degree in social work. For many years, John has been deeply involved in a militant black civil-rights group. His hobbies are photography and collecting civil-rights memorabilia. John is in charge of maintenance for the astrodome experiment.

Volunteer 3: Susan. While female; American; age 56.

Susan is married and has two grown children. She is the general manager of a small factory that produces aids for disabled people. The factory employs seventy-one people. Susan has personally negotiated a large contract for her company and will wrap up final details of the contract when she returns to work. This contract, if signed, would mean employment for an additional eighty-five people. Mary is socially and politically active in her community and is a member of the city council. Her hobby is replicating the techniques of eighteenth-century upholstery, and she intends to write a book on the subject when she retires. Susan's role in the astrodome experiment is to study the group's productivity.

Volunteer 4: Jake. White male; American; age 27.

Jake, who is unmarried, is a physical-education instructor at St. Thomas High School. He joined the army after he graduated from high school and became an infantry-platoon leader during Operation Desert Storm, during which he received a distinguished decoration. He was sent home with a serious shoulder wound from which he has recovered, except for occasional pain. Jake used his military benefits to earn a master's degree in physical education. Since he returned to civilian life, Jake has been unsettled; and his drinking, which is undisclosed, has become a persistent problem. His hobbies are modifying and driving motorcycles. Jake's role in the astrodome experiment is to maintain the group in peak physical condition.

Volunteer 5: Jasmine. Oriental female; Chinese; age 20.

Jasmine, who is single, is a fine-arts student at Harvard University. Her wealthy parents live in Hong Kong, where her father is an industrialist and an international authority on traditional Chinese ceramics. Jasmine is considered extremely attractive and has several well-to-do boyfriends. She recently was among several women who were featured in a television documentary on Asian women. Her role in the astrodome experiment is to write a daily column for the South China Morning Post newspaper on her experience of bringing the traditional Chinese concept of harmony to an isolated community.

Volunteer 6: Louis. White male; French; age 45.

Louis is a medical-research scientist at the university hospital. He is recognized as a world authority on the treatment of malaria. Louis is testing a new, experimental, low-cost malaria treatment, but much of the research data is still in his working notebooks. Louis' hobbies are African music and golf. Louis is divorced and has no children; his ex-wife has remarried, but in the six years since the divorce, he has experienced some emotional difficulties. He has been convicted of indecent exposure twice; the last time was eleven months ago. Louis' role in the astrodome experiment is to act as the expedition's doctor.

ASTRODOME RESCUE RANKING SHEET

Instructions: Your task is to decide the order in which the six trapped astrodome-experiment volunteers are to be rescued. In the blanks provided, write each volunteer's name next to the number that indicates that person's order of rescue.

1. _____

2. _____

3. _____

4. _____

5. _____

6. _____

ASTRODOME RESCUE REVIEW SHEET

Instructions: As a team, discuss the following questions. If sufficient time is available, each member should answer the questions independently before the team's discussion. Record all key points. You do not have to reach consensus; this discussion is purely exploratory.

1. What criteria were used in choosing the order in which the volunteers were to be rescued?
2. How clearly were the criteria expressed? Could this have been done more effectively?
3. How closely did other people's criteria align with your own?
4. How clearly were the values that underlay others' criteria expressed? Could this have been done more effectively?
5. How comfortable did you feel about making this kind of decision? If you felt uncomfortable, why do you think that was so? If the situation had been real, who do you think should have made the decisions?
6. Were there any people in your group with whom you strongly disagreed? Why did you disagree? How do you feel about these people now?
7. What behaviors helped your subgroup to arrive at a decision?
8. What behaviors hindered your subgroup from arriving at a decision?

The New Zin Obelisk[1]

Goals

I. To give the team members the opportunity to experience and examine the sharing of information in team problem solving.

II. To give the team members the opportunity to study leadership, cooperation, and other issues in team problem solving.

Group Size

A team of four to seven members.

Time Required

Approximately fifty minutes.

Materials

I. A copy of The New Zin Obelisk Instruction Sheet and The New Zin Obelisk Review Sheet for each team member.

II. A set of The New Zin Obelisk Information Cards for the team.

III. Blank paper and a pencil for each team member.

IV. A copy of The New Zin Obelisk Answer Sheet for the facilitator's use.

V. A newsprint flip chart and a felt-tipped marker.

Physical Setting

A quiet room in which chairs can be arranged in a circle.

Process

I. The facilitator distributes a copy of The New Zin Obelisk Group Instruction Sheet, blank paper, and a pencil to each team member and instructs the members to read their sheets. (Five minutes.)

---

[1] The authors acknowledge the contribution of Mike Woodcock, co-author of the original version of this activity.

II. The facilitator distributes a set of The New Zin Obelisk Information Cards randomly among the team members and instructs the team to begin the task that was described on the instruction sheets. (Twenty-five minutes.)

III. The facilitator calls time and distributes a copy of The New Zin Obelisk Review Sheet to each team member.

IV. The facilitator reviews the experience with the team members, using the questions on The New Zin Obelisk Review Sheet. (Thirty minutes.)

V. The facilitator lists salient points on a flip chart and, if necessary, the answer and rationale to the problem.

Variations

I. Any number of teams may be directed simultaneously. A set of The New Zin Obelisk Information Cards should be provided for each team.

II. Team members may complete The New Zin Obelisk Review Sheets individually before the group processing takes place.

III. The facilitator may introduce extraneous information to complicate the team's task.

THE NEW ZIN OBELISK INFORMATION CARDS

Instructions: Make a set of thirty 3" x 5" cards for each group, each containing one item of information from the list below. Do not copy the question numbers onto the cards. The cards should be distributed randomly among members of the team.

1. In Atlantis, time is measured in days.
2. Each day is subdivided into wickles and wackles.
3. A *Zin* is a sacred object that is cared for by priests.
4. All Zins are the same size.
5. A Zin is fifty feet in length.
6. A Zin is one hundred feet high.
7. A Zin is ten feet wide.
8. Zins are made of stone blocks.
9. Each stone block measures one cubic foot.
10. Day one in the Atlantean week is called Codday.
11. Day two in the Atlantean week is called Octiday.
12. Day three in the Atlantean week is called Eelday.
13. Day four in the Atlantean week is called Clamday.
14. Day five in the Atlantean week is called Salmonday.
15. There are five days in the Atlantean week.
16. Atlantean workers have a standardized working day.
17. The Atlantean standardized working day has nine wickles, beginning at daybreak.
18. Sixteen wackles of each standardized working day are devoted to rest.
19. There are eight wackles in a wickle.
20. Each worker lays 150 blocks per wickle.
21. There are always nine workers in a gang.
22. One member of the gang is attached to the Atlantean army and does not lay blocks.
23. Every Salmonday is a public holiday.
24. Work on the Zin starts at daybreak on Codday.
25. Only one gang is working on the construction of the Zin.
26. There are eleven gold scales in a gold fin.
27. Each block costs twenty-two gold fins.

28. Bonus payments are made if religious devotions are made as blocks are laid.
29. A shortage of funds means that only three Zins can be constructed this year.
30. An allocation of 30,000 gold fins is available for monuments this year.

THE NEW ZIN OBELISK INSTRUCTION SHEET

In the ancient city of Atlantis, a solid, rectangular obelisk called a *Zin* was built in honor of the goddess Charlotta. The structure took less than two weeks to complete.

The task of your team is to determine on which day of the week the obelisk was completed. You have twenty-five minutes to complete this task. Each team member will be given cards containing information related to building the Zin. You may share this information orally, but you may not show your cards to other team members.

THE NEW ZIN OBELISK ANSWER SHEET

The answer to the problem is *Octiday*.

Rationale

1. The dimensions of the Zin indicate that it contains 50,000 cubic feet of stone blocks.
2. The blocks are one cubic foot each; therefore, 50,000 blocks are required.
3. Each worker works seven wickles per day (two wickles are devoted to rest).
4. Each worker lays 150 blocks per wickle; therefore, each worker lays 1,050 blocks a day.
5. There are eight workers per day; therefore, 8,400 blocks are laid per working day.
6. The fifty-thousandth block, therefore, is laid on the sixth working day.
7. Work started at daybreak on Codday, and as work does not take place on Salmonday, the sixth working day is Octiday.

THE NEW ZIN OBELISK REVIEW SHEET

1. What behaviors helped the team to accomplish its task?
2. What behaviors hindered the team from completing its task?
3. How did leadership emerge in the team?
4. Who participated the most?
5. Who participated the least?
6. What feelings did you experience as the task progressed?
7. What suggestions would you make to improve the team's performance on future tasks involving collaboration?

Activity 16

Role Negotiation[1]

Goals

I. To provide the team members with a structured means of giving task-oriented feedback to one another.

II. To help the team members to work through difficulties in personal and professional relationships.

Time Required

One to two hours for the initial meeting. Several meetings may be required to work through all issues raised by the team members.

Materials

I. Enough copies of the Role Negotiation Message Sheets for each team member to send one to every other member of the team.

II. A pencil for each team member.

Process

I. The facilitator distributes a set of Role Negotiation Message Sheets to each team member. (The number of copies in each set should equal the number of team members minus one.) The facilitator instructs the team members to fill out one message sheet as directed for every other member of the team. (Twenty minutes.)

II. After the team members have completed their message sheets, the facilitator directs them to deliver their sheets to the recipients. (Five minutes.)

III. The team members read the messages that they have received. (Five minutes.)

IV. The facilitator asks the team members to take turns sharing the messages that they have received. The team is instructed to discuss

---

[1] This activity was developed from an idea by Roger Harrison of Development Research Associates.

the messages and is encouraged to give each member feedback on the messages that he or she received, using specific examples if possible. The facilitator encourages the recipients to ask for clarification if necessary and to respond to others' messages with an open mind instead of defensively.

After a discussion about one member's messages is complete, the team members are instructed to break into small groups and, through two-way communication, to negotiate commitments to specific future actions. The facilitator suggests that the members use statements such as "In the future I will...." The facilitator emphasizes that the aim of such negotiations is a "win-win" outcome. The team members are instructed to continue forming small groups and negotiating roles until all the members have met with one another.

(One hour.)

Variation

Statements of commitment to agreed actions can be written on newsprint and posted for the team to view.

ROLE NEGOTIATION MESSAGE SHEET

Message from _____ **to** _____

From my point of view, it would be beneficial if you would...

Do the following things more or better:

Do the following things less, or stop doing them:

Continue doing the following things:

Start doing the following things:

Airplane

Goals

I. To give the team members the opportunity to examine the impact of roles in a team.

II. To develop the members' skills in allocating roles in a team and in distributing the team's work among its members.

Time Required

Two hours.

Group Size

Between twelve and twenty-five people can form one "Airplane" team. Several teams can operate simultaneously.

Materials

I. One copy each of the Airplane Staff Briefing and the Airplane Task Review for each team member.

II. A copy of the Airplane CEO's Briefing Sheet for the person who is assigned that role.

III. One thousand sheets of legal-sized (8½" x 14") paper (scrap may be used), one thousand paper clips, four large rolls of transparent tape, four packets of crayons, ten sheets of 11" x 17" paper, four rulers, and ten pencils for each team.

IV. A video camcorder and a compatible large-screen playback system (if available).

V. A newsprint flip chart and a felt-tipped marker.

Process

I. Before the activity begins, the facilitator prepares the following:

1. A "workshop" that is relatively cramped and unpleasant, including a work table and enough uncomfortable chairs to seat half of the team members. Safety posters, workplace graffiti, and other

typical production-facility materials should be supplied if possible. The sheets of legal-sized paper, transparent tape, crayons, and paper clips should be placed in the workshop.

2. In a separate area, work spaces for the CEO, assistant CEO, and CFO (see Section II), preferably with telephone extensions. The facilities provided should be commensurate with the status of the officers, and every effort should be taken to provide authentic surroundings. The numbers of the telephone extensions should be written on the CEO's briefing sheet.

3. The CEO's briefing sheet should be placed in his or her office. To allow the person who is playing the chief executive officer time to prepare, he or she plus a person to play the role of assistant may be appointed thirty minutes before the other members are assigned roles.

4. The 11" x 17" sheets of paper, rulers, and pencils should be placed in the design office.

II. The facilitator informs the team members that they are about to undertake a role-play experiment in organizing. The facilitator introduces the twelve key roles:

- Chief Executive Officer (CEO)
- Assistant to the Chief Executive Officer
- Chief Financial Officer (CFO)
- Sales Manager
- Head of Design and Development
- Design Engineers (2)
- Workshop Supervisor
- Workshop Operators (4)

The figure on the next page illustrates the organizational structure. As indicated in the figure, if there are more than twelve team members, they may be given roles as the following:

- Additional designers;
- Additional workshop-team staff (supervisors and/or operators);
- A new team of financial auditors that reports to the CFO; or
- A new team of work-study engineers under a manager of work-study engineering, who reports to the CEO.

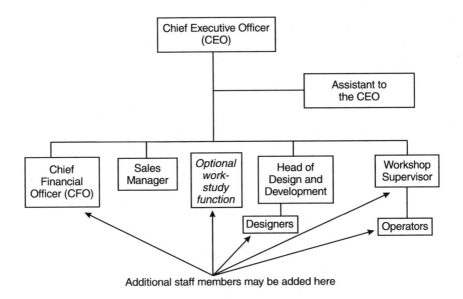

Additional staff members may be added here

The facilitator distributes a copy of the Airplane Staff Briefing to each team member, assigns roles, and instructs the members to begin the role play without further explanation. All members are asked to stay "in character" throughout the role play. (Seventy-five minutes.)

III. During the role play, the facilitator may record the events in all parts of the organization with a video camcorder. The resulting fifteen- to twenty-minute videotape can be shown on a large-screen playback system prior to the process review.

IV. The facilitator introduces the process review by showing the film so that the members can view the events in parts of the organization that they were unable to witness firsthand. The facilitator then instructs the team members to complete the Airplane Review Sheets and to discuss the sheets either as a team or in subgroups of three to five members formed from different parts of the "organization." (Thirty to forty-five minutes).

AIRPLANE CEO'S BRIEFING SHEET

You are the new Chief Executive Officer (CEO) of the Airplane Corporation. Your organization makes paper airplanes and markets them world-wide. Last week your predecessor was caught using company funds at the gambling tables in Las Vegas and is now in jail awaiting trial.

Below is the latest copy of the organizational chart (although the previous CEO is known to have been considering changes that may not be shown on this chart). You may add staff or departments as you wish during the role play.

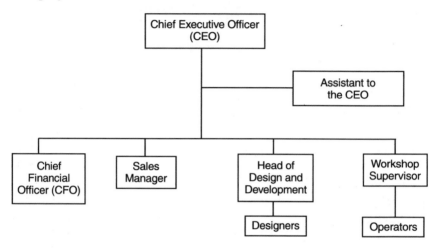

Your staff members, with their phone numbers and locations, are listed below.

	Location	**Phone**
Assistant to the CEO		
CFO		
Sales Manager		
Head of Design and Development		
Designers		
Workshop Supervisor		

The organization currently is idle following the summer shutdown. The work of all departments was completed before the summer vacation commenced. Managers are now getting organized and awaiting instructions as to their next objectives and tasks.

Your Task

You have seventy-five minutes in which to see that your organization achieves the following objectives:

1. Build 300 identical "standard" airplanes that will fly more than four meters (twelve feet);
2. Build 150 identical "budget" airplanes that will fly more than three meters (nine feet) and that are decorated in colors suitable for sale in India, Pakistan, and Thailand;
3. Build fifty identical "special" airplanes that will fly more than three meters (nine feet) and that are suitable for sale in Islamic countries;
4. Build five "experimental" airplanes that make use of innovative thinking;
5. Initiate a program of total quality management (TQM) throughout the organization;
6. Increase operating efficiency by 15 percent each fifteen-minute period;
7. Provide accurate costs for each type of plane; and
8. Conduct a program to make the entire organization more aware of the importance of marketing and sales.

CEO's Rules

1. You may leave your office for a total of only ten minutes during the entire activity, although anyone can come to see you for as long as you wish.
2. You must produce a one-page progress report for *The Wall Street Journal* after the activity has been under way for forty minutes.

AIRPLANE STAFF BRIEFING

You are an employee of the Airplane Corporation, and you are returning from your summer vacation. Before the vacation, all the work of your department was completed.

You read in the newspaper that, last week, the Chief Executive Officer (CEO) of your company was caught using company funds at the gambling tables in Las Vegas and is now in jail awaiting trial.

You are now awaiting instructions from senior management as to your next objectives and tasks. While you are waiting, it is suggested that you prepare to perform your specialized function.

Note: You have been assigned a role and should stay "in character" throughout the activity.

AIRPLANE REVIEW SHEET

Think about the activity that you have just completed and take a few minutes to answer the questions below. After you have finished, discuss your experience with your team members and try to reach some conclusions about how organizations can become more efficient.

1. What are your feelings now?

2. What did you feel during the activity? Why do you think you felt as you did?

3. Who helped the Airplane Corporation to operate effectively? How did the person(s) help?

4. Who hindered the Airplane Corporation from operating effectively? In what ways did the person(s) hinder the operations?

5. How effectively were the roles allocated? How could the role-allocation process have been done more effectively?

6. What have you learned that will help you to be better organized in the future?

Giving Feedback

Goals

   I. To help the team to establish guidelines for giving feedback so that doing so becomes part of the team's culture.

   II. To increase the members' awareness of the importance of developing a team culture that values the giving and receiving of effective feedback.

   III. To give the team members the opportunity to develop their skills in giving and receiving feedback.

Time Required

   One hour and ten minutes.

Materials

   I. A copy of the Giving Feedback Statement Sheet and the Giving Feedback Ranking Sheet for each team member.

   II. A pencil for each team member.

   III. A newsprint flip chart and a felt-tipped marker.

Process

   I. The facilitator distributes a Giving Feedback Statement Sheet, a Giving Feedback Ranking Sheet, and a pencil to each team member and invites the members to complete the task as directed. (Fifteen minutes.)

Note: This activity enables a team to evaluate its approach to giving and receiving feedback. Therefore, it is a prerequisite for later activities in this book in which giving and receiving feedback is a significant element. These activities are identified by the symbol *F* in the Index to Activities.

II. Each team member is asked to present his or her selection of five priority statements to the group and to state briefly why each one is important. (Twenty minutes.)

III. The facilitator lists the numbers that correspond to each member's priority statements on newsprint and leads the team in a discussion of which priority statements are most significant to the team and which ones should be omitted (if any). (Thirty minutes.)

IV. After the team has reached consensus on a list of priorities, the facilitator records the priorities on newsprint under the following heading:

For this team, good feedback is:

(Five minutes.)

V. Before the team undertakes any other activities that involve the giving of feedback, the newsprint poster that was prepared in Step IV should be displayed and reviewed.

GIVING FEEDBACK STATEMENT SHEET

Your Task

Read the notes on giving and receiving feedback below. When you have finished, select the five statements from the list of nine that are the most important to you when you are receiving feedback.

List your five statements in order of importance on the Giving Feedback Ranking Sheet. Include a brief rationale for each ranking.

What Is Feedback?

The giving and receiving of feedback is one of the most significant methods of assisting personal growth. When asked to identify some of the most important experiences in their personal development, most people will talk about others who have given them direct and pertinent information about themselves. Such feedback can have so much impact that it can profoundly influence the ways in which people behave.

Feedback is a powerful tool and can be abused. People sometimes are hurt or insulted because of ill-intentioned or poorly phrased feedback. The intention of the giver of feedback should never be to hurt, ridicule, or "get back at" the recipient. If feedback is given correctly, the recipient becomes stronger and more effective.

Criteria for Giving and Receiving Feedback

To be effective, feedback should be:

1. *Given with care.* The giver of feedback should care for the recipient. The giver's intention should be to help, not to hurt.
2. *Given with attention.* The giver of feedback needs to be aware of the recipient's responses—both verbal and nonverbal. A giver of feedback should also be a good listener.
3. *Invited by the recipient.* Feedback is most effective when the recipient has invited it. A person who has asked for feedback is likely to be more open to identifying and exploring particular areas of concern.
4. *Specific and behavioral.* Good feedback is specific and deals with *behavior* that the recipient can change. Vague statements such as "Your arrogance annoys me" are of little value. "When I greet you and you ignore me, I feel slighted" is specific and addresses an action that can be changed. The most useful feedback is direct, open, and concrete.

5. *Fully expressed.* Effective feedback requires more than a bald statement of facts. Feelings also need to be expressed so that the recipient can judge the full impact of his or her behavior.

6. *Uncluttered by judgment.* Feedback that is composed of judgments or evaluations often is accusatory in tone and is likely to make the recipient react defensively. If a judgment must be made, the giver of feedback should state clearly that his or her opinion is subjective, describe the situation as he or she sees it, and allow the recipient to make the evaluation.

7. *Well timed.* The most useful feedback is given when the receiver is receptive to it and when the behavior or event is fresh in his or her mind. It is *not* helpful for the giver of feedback to "store up" angry feelings and to let them out all at once.

8. *Directed toward changeable behavior.* The most useful feedback concerns behavior that can be changed. Feedback that addresses matters that are beyond the recipient's control is less useful. It often is helpful for the giver to suggest ways in which the recipient could change his or her behavior; this may give the recipient new ideas for solving old problems.

9. *Checked and clarified.* If possible, a person should check his or her perceptions with others to find out if they are shared before giving feedback. This is especially important in a training group and also can be utilized in work teams. After others' viewpoints are collected and assimilated, the person may perceive the offending behavior more objectively.

GIVING FEEDBACK RANKING SHEET

Statement number   **Why I think it is important**

Pluses and Minuses

Goals[1]

I. To identify the strengths and weaknesses of a team's performance over a specified period.

II. To give the team members the opportunity to reach consensus on ways that they can reinforce the positive aspects and overcome the negative aspects of their team's performance.

Time Required

One hour and fifteen minutes.

Materials

I. A copy of the Pluses and Minuses Activity Sheet for each team member.

II. A pencil for each team member.

III. A newsprint flip chart and at least three felt-tipped markers, each a different color.

Process

I. The facilitator distributes a Pluses and Minuses Activity Sheet and a pencil to each team member and asks the members to read their sheets. (Five minutes.)

II. The facilitator instructs the team members to choose a period of time for which they will evaluate the team's performance (three months is suggested). Team members are directed to complete the Pluses and Minuses Activity Sheet. (Fifteen minutes.)

---

[1] The facilitator should be aware that this activity is confrontational and should be undertaken only with team members who volunteer to participate. It is especially important that the facilitator does not react in a defensive manner. A team that is relatively new to team building should consider Activity 18, "Giving Feedback," to be a prerequisite to this activity.

III. The team members are instructed to decide whether they will sign their sheets or submit them anonymously. (Five minutes.)

IV. One person (the facilitator or a team member) copies all of the items in full onto a newsprint sheet. The team identifies the items on which members agree and either transfers them to another newsprint sheet or highlights them with a different-colored marker. The team members then discuss the areas in which there are differences and attempt to reach a consensus evaluation. Unresolved items should be left for discussion on another occasion. It is important that the facilitator limit the time that the members spend on this step. (Fifteen minutes.)

V. The positive aspects of the team's performance are ranked in terms of their contributions to the effectiveness of the team. (Ten minutes.)

VI. The negative aspects of the team's performance are ranked in terms of how much they *detract* from (or fail to contribute to) the effectiveness of the team. (Ten minutes.)

VII. The facilitator instructs the team members to determine three actions that they will take in the next month that will reduce the negative factors and three actions that they will take to reinforce or improve the positive factors. (Twenty minutes.)

PLUSES AND MINUSES ACTIVITY SHEET

Your name (optional): _____

Period under review: _____

During the period under review, the five best things this team has achieved are:

1.

2.

3.

4.

5.

During the period under review, the five areas in which this team has not performed well are:

1.

2.

3.

4.

5.

People-Skills Inventory[1]

Goals

    I. To provide the members of the team with a systematic basis for self-evaluation and for team feedback on individual managemenet skills.

    II. To identify team members' priorities for the development of management skills.

Time Required

    A minimum of one hour.

Materials

    I. A copy of the People-Skills Inventory and the People-Skills Inventory Summary Sheet for each team member.

    II. A pencil for each team member.

Process

    I. The facilitator distributes the People-Skills Inventory, the People-Skills Inventory Summary Sheet, and a pencil to each team member and instructs the members to complete the inventory. (Fifteen minutes.)

    II. The facilitator invites the team members to share their scores with the team. Members should take turns receiving feedback from the group (about fifteen minutes per person usually is adequate). The facilitator instructs the team members to follow the guidelines for giving and receiving feedback that were outlined in Activity 18, "Giving Feedback."

---

[1] Adapted from A.G. Banet, "Consultation-Skills Inventory," in J.W. Pfeiffer and J.E. Jones (Eds.), *The 1976 Annual Handbook for Group Facilitators*. San Diego, CA: Pfeiffer & Company, 1976.

Variation

A large team can be divided into subgroups, each with three or four members, for Step II.

PEOPLE-SKILLS INVENTORY

This inventory is designed to help you think about important interpersonal behaviors. You will have the opportunity to review your own behavior and skills.

Instructions: Think about how much you currently practice the behavior listed for each item. If you think that you currently practice the behavior *an appropriate amount,* place a check mark (✓) on the blank in the "Satisfied with status quo" column. If you think that you want or need to practice the behavior *more,* place a check mark on the blank in the "Need to do this more" column. If you think that you want or need to practice the behavior *less,* place a check mark on the blank in the "Need to do this less" column.

Some behaviors that are important to you may not be listed here. Blanks are provided at the end of each section for you to add behaviors and to rank yourself accordingly.

If you wish, you may ignore items that are not relevant to your current situation.

	Satisfied with status quo	Need to do this more	Need to do this less
Assertiveness			
1. Competing with my peers	_____	_____	_____
2. Being open with my superiors	_____	_____	_____
3. Feeling inferior to colleagues	_____	_____	_____
4. Standing up for myself	_____	_____	_____
5. Building open relationships	_____	_____	_____
6. Following policy guidelines	_____	_____	_____
7. Questioning policy guidelines	_____	_____	_____
and _____	_____	_____	_____
and _____	_____	_____	_____
My Team			
8. Getting to know my team members as individuals	_____	_____	_____
9. Meeting with my team a sufficient amount of time	_____	_____	_____
10. Supporting open expression of views	_____	_____	_____

	Satisfied with status quo	Need to do this more	Need to do this less
11. Setting high standards	_____	_____	_____
12. Confronting behavior that deviates from the team norm	_____	_____	_____
13. Clarifying aims and objectives	_____	_____	_____
14. Presenting my views	_____	_____	_____
15. Using my status to influence team decisions	_____	_____	_____
16. Delegating to reduce my workload	_____	_____	_____
and _____	_____	_____	_____
and _____	_____	_____	_____

One-on-One Relationships

	Satisfied with status quo	Need to do this more	Need to do this less
17. Helping others to recognize problems	_____	_____	_____
18. Counseling others	_____	_____	_____
19. Being distant with some people	_____	_____	_____
20. Intervening when things go wrong	_____	_____	_____
21. Being strong when I reprimand others	_____	_____	_____
22. Giving energy to others	_____	_____	_____
23. Clarifying people's objectives	_____	_____	_____
24. Supporting others when they are troubled	_____	_____	_____
25. Bringing problems out in the open	_____	_____	_____
26. Supporting risk taking by others	_____	_____	_____
27. Openly communicating my assessment of another's performance	_____	_____	_____
and _____	_____	_____	_____
and _____	_____	_____	_____

Relationships with Others in the Organization

	Satisfied with status quo	Need to do this more	Need to do this less
28. Letting employees get to know me	_____	_____	_____
29. Being available to employees	_____	_____	_____

	Satisfied with status quo	Need to do this more	Need to do this less
30. Knowing how people feel	_____	_____	_____
31. Acting early to resolve conflicts	_____	_____	_____
32. Communicating both good news and bad news	_____	_____	_____
33. Communicating information quickly	_____	_____	_____
34. Demonstrating my personal status	_____	_____	_____
35. Bypassing managerial structure when communicating	_____	_____	_____
and _____	_____	_____	_____
and _____	_____	_____	_____

Working in Groups

	Satisfied with status quo	Need to do this more	Need to do this less
36. Using a structured approach to manage meetings	_____	_____	_____
37. Developing others' skills in groups	_____	_____	_____
38. Being prompt	_____	_____	_____
39. Using time effectively	_____	_____	_____
40. Listening actively	_____	_____	_____
41. Expressing my views openly	_____	_____	_____
42. Dominating others	_____	_____	_____
43. Maintaining a positive group climate	_____	_____	_____
44. Dealing with disruptive behavior in a constructive manner	_____	_____	_____
45. Forging informal contacts with each member of the team	_____	_____	_____
46. Forging contacts with other teams with which we are interdependent	_____	_____	_____
47. Sharing objectives with other teams	_____	_____	_____
48. Identifying mutual communication needs with other teams	_____	_____	_____
49. Arranging intergroup team-building events	_____	_____	_____

	Satisfied with status quo	Need to do this more	Need to do this less
50. Acting to resolve conflicts between teams	_____	_____	_____
and _____	_____	_____	_____
and _____	_____	_____	_____

Training and Development

	Satisfied with status quo	Need to do this more	Need to do this less
51. Making time to counsel others	_____	_____	_____
52. Making time to receive counseling from others	_____	_____	_____
53. Giving coaching assignments	_____	_____	_____
54. Allocating resources for training	_____	_____	_____
55. Giving feedback to others	_____	_____	_____
56. Sharing parts of my job so that others may continue their professional development	_____	_____	_____
and _____	_____	_____	_____
and _____	_____	_____	_____

Self-Development

	Satisfied with status quo	Need to do this more	Need to do this less
57. Setting aside time to think	_____	_____	_____
58. Visiting similar organizations that have a reputation for excellence	_____	_____	_____
59. Clarifying the underlying principles and values by which I operate	_____	_____	_____
60. Taking on new challenges	_____	_____	_____
61. Attending training events	_____	_____	_____
62. Knowing when and how to use specialized resources	_____	_____	_____
and _____	_____	_____	_____
and _____	_____	_____	_____

PEOPLE-SKILLS INVENTORY SUMMARY SHEET

Instructions: Review your completed People-Skills Inventory and your responses. Select the three or four practices that you most want to change (either by doing them more or doing them less). List the practices in the spaces provided below and discuss your assessments with others. Complete the third column ("How") during your discussion.

BEHAVIORS THAT I WISH TO IMPROVE	WHY	HOW
1.		
2.		
3.		
4.		

Good Coaching Practice

Goals

I. To give the team members the opportunity to identify and practice the skills involved in coaching.

II. To help the team members to develop a "coaching climate."

Time Required

Approximately one hour.

Materials

I. One copy of the Good Coaching Practice Checklist and a pencil for each team member.

II. A newsprint flip chart and a felt-tipped marker.

III. Masking tape for posting newsprint.

Physical Setting

A room large enough to accommodate a circle of chairs for the team members. The room should be large enough to give subgroups some measure of privacy.

Process

I. The facilitator explains that the purpose of the activity is to help the team to identify the characteristics of good coaching. Coaching is defined as *intentionally helping another person to improve his or her competence by utilizing opportunities for development on the job.* The facilitator writes this definition on a sheet of newsprint and displays the newsprint as a reminder during the session.

II. If the team is large enough, the facilitator divides the team members into subgroups (with three or four members in each subgroup) and asks that each subgroup seat its members in a circle and separate the circles to allow some privacy.

III. The facilitator distributes a copy of the Good Coaching Practice Checklist and a pencil to each team member.

IV. The facilitator invites the subgroups to read the checklist instructions and to complete the assignment. (Thirty minutes.)

V. The facilitator instructs the subgroup members to reconvene as a team and to share their lists with one another. Using a "master list" prepared on a newsprint poster, the facilitator tallies the items that the members have deleted and adds any items that the members suggest. (Ten minutes.)

VI. The facilitator asks the members to reach consensus on the final version of their checklist. (Twenty minutes.)

VII. The facilitator has the final checklist typed and titles it "Our Guidelines for Coaching." He or she distributes a copy to each team member.

VIII. After the team has created its framework for assessing coaching sessions, further understanding and skills can be acquired with practice. One way that the leader can continue to develop the members' skills is to invite an observer(s) to watch the team's coaching sessions, using the team's checklist and giving the team members feedback after the sessions. This step can be successful only if the voluntary agreement of all team members who will participate in coaching sessions is obtained.

GOOD COACHING PRACTICE CHECKLIST

Instructions: Listed below are eighteen characteristics that are considered factors in effective on-the-job coaching. For the purpose of this exercise, coaching is defined as *intentionally helping another person to improve his or her competence by utilizing opportunities for development on the job.*

Your group's task is to develop a checklist of coaching behaviors that is appropriate to your situation. You may not agree that every item is significant for you. If you decide that a behavior is not helpful for you, draw a line through it. As the list is incomplete, you may wish to add additional statements of coaching characteristics. Write these items in the blanks provided at the end of the list.

1. Before any meeting, opportunities for coaching are listed systematically by the coach.

2. Before any meeting, opportunities for coaching are listed systematically by the person who will be coached.

3. The coaching discussion begins by both parties' checking out what the other is seeking to achieve.

4. Clear objectives are set for the coaching process.

5. A written contract for the coaching process is produced.

6. Explicit success criteria are set for the coaching process.

7. The coach observes the other person's behavior in critical situations.

8. Feelings can be expressed openly.

9. Problems are analyzed jointly.

10. Options for action are identified, and their benefits and drawbacks are evaluated explicitly.

11. There is a strong emphasis on action.

12. Opportunities for personal development are sought out.

13. The coach spends much of the coaching session practicing active listening.

14. The coach spends about 25 percent of the coaching session giving advice.

15. The coaching discussions are confidential.

16. Steps are taken to prevent interruptions during coaching sessions.

17. Each meeting is reviewed so that both participants can learn from the experience.

18. A date for the next meeting always is established for follow-up.

Team Brainstorming

Goals

I. To give the team members the opportunity to practice a proven method of generating creative ideas.

II. To develop the members' skills in creative problem solving.

III. To improve the effectiveness of team meetings.

Group Size

Between three and eight members. Larger teams should be divided into appropriately sized subgroups.

Time Required

One hour.

Materials

I. A newsprint flip chart and a felt-tipped marker.

II. Masking tape for posting newsprint.

Process

I. The facilitator writes the five basic rules for brainstorming on a sheet of newsprint before the session commences:

1. There will be no criticism (either stated or implied) during the brainstorming session.

2. All ideas, no matter how ridiculous they may seem at first, are encouraged.

3. As many ideas as possible should be generated.

4. Ideas should be built on (used as stepping stones to other ideas) by other people whenever possible.

5. Brainstorming must continue for the allotted time even if the ideas temporarily "dry up."

II. The facilitator introduces the activity by outlining the purpose of the session and by describing his or her role. The facilitator has seven key functions in a brainstorming session:

1. To structure the work of the group(s);
2. To introduce and explain brainstorming techniques;
3. To capture and record ideas as they are generated;
4. To prevent the team from evaluating ideas until the appropriate stage;
5. To empower the team members to be creative;
6. To assist the team members in moving toward well-defined outcomes; and
7. To demonstrate how the training experience can be applied to actual situations.

III. The facilitator presents the five basic rules for brainstorming as outlined in Step I.

IV. The facilitator gives the team members a task and tells them to brainstorm possible solutions. The following are suggested brainstorming tasks that the facilitator can use as is or to spark his or her own creativity:

- How to make this team operate better
- How to encourage and allow more reticent members to participate in team meetings
- How to plan meeting agendas for the most efficient use of the team members' time
- How to reduce the number of muggings and pickpocketings in large cities
- How to give teenagers a constructive summer vacation
- How to design cities in the Twenty-First Century
- How to reduce the costs of running the police force without reducing its efficiency
- How to save resources in the home
- How to increase the possibility that children will enjoy visits to the dentist
- How to entertain staff members during the lunch hour

The facilitator lists all of the members' ideas on newsprint. (Five minutes.)

V. The facilitator invites the team members to make initial evaluations of the ideas that were generated, using the following process:

1. Cluster ideas that are similar.
2. Evaluate the ideas in terms of value/benefit, cost, feasibility, and resources needed to enact.

(Twenty minutes.)

VI. The facilitator posts the final listing of evaluated ideas and asks the team to rank order the ideas according to their feasibility. (Five minutes.)

VII. A second practice session is held on the topic of using the brainstorming technique in team meetings. (Thirty minutes.)

Creative Attitudes

Goals

I. To give the team members the opportunity to explore attitudes that help or hinder the expression of creative ideas.

II. To improve the creativity of team meetings.

Group Size

A team (or several subgroups) of four to seven members each.

Time Required

One hour to one hour and fifteen minutes.

Materials

I. A copy of the Creative Attitudes Individual Task Sheet for each team member.

II. A copy of the Creative Attitudes Group Task Sheet for the team (or for each subgroup).

III. A pencil for each team member.

IV. A newsprint flip chart and a felt-tipped marker.

V. Masking tape for posting newsprint.

Physical Setting

A room in which the team members can be seated comfortably. If there are to be subgroups, each subgroup should have its own room.

Process

I. The facilitator introduces the activity by outlining the purpose of the session. The facilitator distributes the Creative Attitudes Individual Task Sheets and pencils to the members and asks them to work individually to complete the task as directed. (Fifteen minutes.)

II. The facilitator distributes a copy of the Creative Attitudes Group Task Sheet to the team (or to each subgroup) and instructs the members to work together to complete the task outlined. (Forty minutes.)

III. The team or the subgroups are asked to share and discuss their results. (Fifteen minutes.)

IV. The facilitator concludes the session by asking the team members to discuss which of the principles that they have discussed are relevant on the job. The facilitator records key points on newsprint; these notes are typed up and handed out to the members after the session. (Ten minutes.)

CREATIVE ATTITUDES INDIVIDUAL TASK SHEET

A team's level of creativity is greatly affected by its psychological climate. You are asked to determine the characteristics of a creative psychological climate by doing the following:

1. Reflect on your own experiences in creative groups.
2. Consider the twenty statements below.
3. Select five statements that you believe are the most significant to the sustenance of a team's creative psychological climate.
4. Rank the five statements that you selected in order of importance to you as a team member.

A team is more creative when...

1. Meetings are run in a structured fashion.
2. It is recognized that almost everyone can be truly creative.
3. Time is set aside to allow new ideas to surface.
4. Discontent is perceived as positive.
5. Members prefer trying new things to perfecting old ones.
6. Small creative steps are considered as important as (and often contribute to) large-scale innovations.
7. Conflict is considered to help the creative process.
8. Having fun is perceived as essential to creativity.
9. Fear of failure does not inhibit creativity.
10. The effective marketing of an idea is as important as having a good idea in the first place.
11. An opportunity to think is an essential part of the creative process.
12. It sometimes feels "stuck."
13. Members go for quantity when they are generating ideas.
14. Ideas are not evaluated until all the creative possibilities have been explored.
15. Anyone can make a creative contribution, even to specialized issues.
16. Many truly useful ideas come from customers.
17. Joint projects with customers (internal or external) are considered good ways to promote creativity.
18. Ideas tend to form as pictures rather than as words.
19. It uses mistakes as teaching tools.
20. It utilizes the creativity of individual members.

CREATIVE ATTITUDES GROUP TASK SHEET

You each have spent some time exploring the characteristics of a creative group psychological climate by considering your experience. In your team or subgroup, you will now think of ways to make your team's psychological climate more creative.

In your team or subgroup, take turns sharing your responses to the Creative Attitudes Individual Task Sheet and explaining your underlying thinking.

After you have finished, complete the following phrases as a group.

We would have a more creative team if...

The team leader did these things differently:

Team members did these things differently:

The following techniques were used in team meetings:

Castles in the Air

Goals

I. To give the team members the opportunity to clarify the processes that are essential for the achievement of creative tasks.

II. To give the team members the opportunity to explore the dynamics of interteam relationships.

Group Size

At least two, but not more than six, teams of four to seven members each. (This activity is particularly useful when the teams consist of members from different work units or departments in the same organization.)

Time Required

Two hours.

Materials

I. One Castle-Building Kit, containing the following items, for each team:

- One package of paper table napkins
- One pair of scissors
- One dozen assorted buttons
- One ball of string
- One package of paper baking cups
- One box of crayons
- One roll of transparent tape
- One hundred 3" x 5" index cards
- One hundred 5" x 7" index cards
- Four ping-pong balls
- One box of large paper clips

- Fifty pipe cleaners
- One packet of assorted balloons (each team should receive the same number of balloons).

II. A copy of the Castles in the Air Task Sheet and the Castles in the Air Review Sheet for each team member.

III. A newsprint flip chart and a felt-tipped marker for each team.

IV. Masking tape for posting newsprint.

Physical Setting

A room large enough for the teams to meet and work without distracting one another, or one large meeting room plus a separate room for each team. A good-sized work table is required for each team.

Process

I. The facilitator instructs the members to form teams, then distributes a Castle-Building Kit to each team and a copy of the Castles in the Air Task Sheet to each team member.

II. The facilitator instructs the team members to read the task sheets and to complete the assignment as described. Each team is given space (or a separate room) in which to construct a castle. If desired, an observer may be designated for each team, or the teams' activities may be videotaped. (One hour.)

III. The facilitator designates each team with a letter: "A, B, C," and so on. The facilitator tells the members that each team will spend the next five minutes examining another team's castle and evaluating it for imaginative effort. No further definition of "imaginative effort" is given. Team A will evaluate Team B's castle, Team B will evaluate Team C's castle, and so on, with the last team evaluating Team A's castle. The facilitator tells the teams that they may use their own criteria for evaluation. (Five minutes.)

IV. The facilitator announces that each team is to select one member who will join the team whose castle has just been evaluated to assist it in improving its model. (Twenty minutes.)

V. The final castles are displayed. The facilitator instructs the participants to form groups of four, each group including a representative from each project team. The groups are instructed to analyze their methods of completing the project by discussing the following questions:

1. How well did your team function during the initial problem-solving task?

2. How did you feel about the other team's evaluation of your castle?

3. How did the representative from the evaluation group affect your team?

4. How do you regard the evaluation team now?

(Twenty minutes.)

VI. Each team reassembles to analyze individual results, to review either the observer's notes or the videotape of its process, and to complete the assignment as defined on the Castles in the Air Review Sheet. The facilitator provides each team with a newsprint flip chart and a felt-tipped marker. (Thirty minutes.)

VII. Each team makes a presentation and displays its chart. (Five minutes.)

CASTLES IN THE AIR TASK SHEET

Using only the materials in the Castle-Building Kit, construct a castle that stands at least two feet tall. Make your castle as imaginative as possible. You have one hour to complete this assignment.

CASTLES IN THE AIR REVIEW SHEET

Reflecting on your experience in general and during this activity, identify several factors that you believe help or hinder intergroup relationships. Working in your team, use this information to prepare a five-minute presentation, illustrated with cartoons, for the other team(s). You have thirty minutes for your review and to prepare your cartoon presentation.

```
┌─────────────────┐
│ Activity 25     │
└─────────────────┘
```

Interteam Mapping

Goals

I. To give the team members the opportunity to define their team's position within the broader organization.

II. To give the team members the opportunity to explore the nature of defined organizational relationships.

Time Required

Approximately two hours.

Materials

I. A copy of the Interteam Mapping Task Sheet for each team member.

II. A newsprint flip chart and at least three colors of felt-tipped markers.

III. Masking tape for posting newsprint.

Physical Setting

A room with enough wall space to post newsprint sheets.

Process

I. The facilitator explains that a "map" will be drawn to explore the team's relationships with other teams. The facilitator draws a circle in the center of a sheet of newsprint and explains that the circle represents the team.

II. The team members are asked to identify other work units within the organization with which they interact. The facilitator draws smaller circles on the newsprint sheet to represent these other work units.

III. The team members are asked to discuss their relationships with the other groups. The facilitator diagrams the relationships on the newsprint sheet, using the instructions provided on the task sheet.

INTERTEAM MAPPING TASK SHEET

Your Task: Draw a "map" to illustrate your team's relationships with other teams. The figure below is an example.

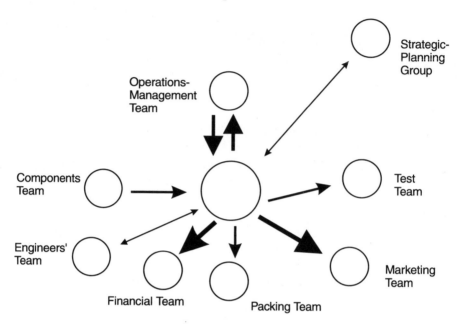

Sample Interteam Map

1. Draw a circle in the center of a sheet of newsprint. This circle represents your team.

2. Draw other circles on the newsprint sheet to represent the other teams with which your team interacts.

3. In your team, discuss your team's relationships with other teams and diagram the significance of the relationships by drawing arrows of different thicknesses to indicate the levels of interaction and their importance. (The above example represents the most basic "map.") Colors may be used to represent various flows of communication (e.g., exchanges of materials, of information, or of specialized services).

4. The nature of the relationship (e.g., input to or output from) can be symbolized with the use of directional arrows at the end of the relationship lines.

5. If necessary, each relationship line can be numbered; and comments on the nature of the relationships, their purposes, and their appropriateness can be listed on a separate sheet of newsprint.

6. Each member should check the map to ensure that there is consensus and that no groups have been omitted.

7. Discuss the following questions:

- Are there any other parts of the organization with which we need more interaction? improved interaction? to commence or cease interaction?

- What specific things would we like to do in order to provide better service? receive better service? make our interactions more useful or positive?

- Is action a matter for the team's leader, for the entire team, or for certain team members?

8. The map can be shared with other teams as a means of communicating specific views about mutual interactions.

9. The map can be used as the starting point in creating a priority list of actions that the team can take to improve its relationships with other parts of the organization.

Editor: Jennifer O. Bryant
Editorial Assistants: Heidi Erika Callinan and Katharine Munson
Page Composition and Interior Design: Judy Whalen
Cover Design: Heather Kennedy

This book was edited and formatted using 486 platforms with 8MB RAM and high-resolution, dual-page monitors. The copy was produced using Word-Perfect software; pages composed with Ventura software; illustrations produced in Corel Draw. The text is set in thirteen on fifteen Century Schoolbook and heads are Stone Serif Bold and Bold Italic. Camera-ready copy was output on a 1200-dpi laser imagesetter by Pfeiffer and Company.